AF324666

Understanding Brexit Options

What future for Britain?

David Kauders

Sparkling Books

British Library Cataloguing in Publication Data. A catalogue record for this book is available from the British Library.

Edited by Sue Merron

Cover design Rosangela Cuffaro / iStock.com / CharlieAJA

Author photo: Daniela Fricke

Printed by Createspace

2.1

Acknowledgements

Data taken from House of Commons Library research briefings: contains Parliamentary information licensed under the **Open Parliament Licence v3.0.**

During the summer and early-autumn months of 2016 in which this book was written, the UK press and media have carried extensive coverage of Brexit-related issues. Many individual points have appeared in more than one source. Apart from specific references that appear in the text, it would be inappropriate to attribute particular items to individual sources. The author would like to thank all the media for the extent of their collective coverage. The author also thanks everyone who has helped with this book for their dedication to Britain.

The author

David Kauders FRSA was educated at Latymer Upper School, Jesus College Cambridge and Cranfield School of Management. He is an investment manager and also contributes occasional articles to the UK financial press.

Wisdom from our forebears

"A bird in the hand is worth two in the bush"

– proverb

"[He] warns the heads of parties against believing their own lies"

– Dr John Arbuthnot (1667-1735)

"Men, it has been well said, think in herds; it will be seen that they go mad in herds, while they only recover their senses slowly, and one by one."

– Extraordinary Popular Delusions and the Madness of Crowds,
Charles Mackay, preface to 1852 edition

"Just the place for a Snark!" the Bellman cried,
As he landed his crew with care;
Supporting each man on the top of the tide
By a finger entwined in his hair.

"Just the place for a Snark! I have said it twice:
That alone should encourage the crew.
Just the place for a Snark! I have said it thrice:
What I tell you three times is true."

– The Hunting of the Snark, Lewis Carroll

"... they display in particular only a slight aptitude for reasoning, the absence of a critical spirit, irritability, credulity, and simplicity. In their decision, moreover, is to be traced the influence of the leaders of crowds and the part played by ... affirmation, repetition, prestige and contagion."

– Psychology of Crowds,
Gustave le Bon, 'Electoral crowds'

Table of Contents

Abbreviations

For brevity, I have used the following expressions:

- "UK" for the United Kingdom of Great Britain and Northern Ireland (Royaume-Uni), which I also refer to as "Britain";
- "EU" for the European Union (L'Union Européenne);
- "EFTA" for the European Free Trade Association (Norway, Iceland, Liechtenstein and Switzerland);
- "EEA" for the countries that are party to the European Economic Area Agreement (also known as the **single market**), namely all 28 EU member states (including the UK) **plus** Norway, Iceland and Liechtenstein;
- "UKIP" for the United Kingdom Independence Party;
- "SNP" for the Scottish National Party; and
- "GDP" for Gross Domestic Product, a common measure of the size of a country's economy.

Other abbreviations are explained when first used.

I also use the jargon word "Brexiter" to mean anyone encouraging Britain to leave the EU, whether or not they held or hold any formal role within any specific campaign or political party.

List of tables

For clarity, tables 1, 2 and 5 can be downloaded from www.sparklingbooks.com/brexit.html

Introduction

This book grew out of some private research about Britain's relationship with Europe. Given the risks to the British economy, to the unity of the United Kingdom and to European cooperation, I thought it useful to rewrite it and extend it a little. My aim is to provide information and enable the reader to draw logical conclusions, and therefore I have avoided an academic study.

Chapter 1 is the key that unlocks the door and therefore the main part of the book. It explains the options that Britain now has. These options need to be understood before Britain commits to any particular course of action. Because these options are so important, they appear first, with the supporting detail following in later chapters.

Chapter 2 discusses Britain's trade issues in more detail and shows how errors and misconceptions have surfaced. Chapter 3 covers the non-trade factors, notably how to reunite the United Kingdom following the divisive referendum campaign. Chapter 4 deals with Britain's mishandled relationship with Europe, chapter 5 looks at the state of the UK and chapter 6 summarises the main points and deals with the immediate issue: what now?

The anti-establishment feeling that is now manifesting itself throughout Europe, as in the United States, can be traced to the failure of Keynesian economic stimulus as the limit to debt creation is reached, together with a new economic cycle driven by central bank monetary policies. I call the limit to debt creation the "financial system limit" and the reader will find this and related economic topics discussed in my other books.

The evidence presented in this book shows that Britain should stay inside the single market and inside the customs union. If you disagree with this analysis, do at least read this book to understand why Britain has such difficult choices to make.

David Kauders

October 2016

1 Britain's options

Although the British people spoke on 23rd June 2016 and said "we don't feel European", it has become clear that the voting public and those spearheading the Vote Leave campaign were confused about what they voted for. There was no plan because Vote Leave did not expect to win and neither Brexiters nor the civil service had anything in place.

Despite the appearance of a return to normality with a new British prime minister, there is little evidence that anyone has a clue about what Britain should do now to prevent future economic damage from loss of trade. This book sets out a view of what the options appear to be. Two of the options are fairly standard in terms of European law and existing arrangements between nations; two others need individual design.

A good leader will get all alternatives out into the open and attempt to quantify each one of them. Good strategy can be formed by balancing the quantitative case with the qualitative, political and emotional cases before taking any action.

The four options are:

1. "Hard Brexit", a complete break with the European Union.

2. A "loose arrangement" requiring continuing negotiation which attempts to mitigate the worst problems with Hard Brexit.

3. "Soft Brexit", staying in the single market as a non-EU associate (which may be inside or outside the EU customs union) – this is sometimes called "Brexit-lite."

4. A Close Association agreement within the single market and customs union.

Timetable for the UK to leave the EU

Article 50 of the Lisbon treaty was drafted in the expectation that it would never be used. The opening words are:

1. "Any Member State may decide to withdraw from the Union in accordance with its own constitutional requirements.

2. "A Member State which decides to withdraw shall notify the European Council of its intention. In the light of the guidelines provided by the European Council, the Union shall negotiate and conclude an agreement with that State, setting out the arrangements for its withdrawal, taking account of the framework for its future relationship with the Union."

The key words here are "shall negotiate and conclude an agreement ... taking account of the framework for its future relationship." This means that negotiations about the future relationship ought to be separate from exit negotiations.

Britain has to give notice that it is leaving the EU, using Article 50 of the Lisbon treaty that sets the two-year exit clock running. Once this notice is given, Britain loses all negotiating power, which is why the rest of the EU are saying "no negotiations until you give Article 50 notice."

Article 50 goes on to specify that the remaining member states will decide what terms to offer, which can then be agreed by qualified majority in the European council and approved by the European parliament. This prevents any one EU member state blocking them, although the parliament might do so. However, negotiating Britain's ongoing relationship may need a new treaty between the United Kingdom and the other 27 EU member states, which would give every one of the 27 a blocking vote and could take more than a year to ratify once negotiated. This means that such an arrangement must not disrupt any key EU principle such as the four freedoms (see chapter 2), nor must it fall foul of national politics such as Spain's desire not to encourage separatist movements. It should be obvious that the increasing climate of distrust between London and Brussels makes the chance of negotiating such a treaty and ratifying it within two years exactly nil. This strengthens the case for being clear about what Britain wants, and obtaining support for it throughout the United Kingdom, before giving notice. It also strengthens the case for the simplest possible Brexit. Otherwise, the remaining 27 member states may spin the process out, refuse any extension, and leave Britain with nothing.

Option 1, a complete break with the EU: "Hard Brexit"

The first option is to completely exit the EU, including exiting the single market. There will be only limited negotiation, because the terms will be forced upon Britain. This option would cause obvious disruption: no free movement from exit day, so no passporting of services, which would send work for banks, insurers and airlines straight to other countries, damaging industries relying on imported labour (construction, food processing, security guards, cleaners and care workers) and resulting in even longer waiting times for National Health Service (NHS) appointments as staff depart or choose not to come to Britain to further their careers.

This is the option favoured by UKIP and the extreme right wing of the Conservative party. It causes the maximum damage to Britain's trade, because changing from European trading partners to distant nations will be extremely disruptive for a decade or more.

Hard Brexit and the single market
Britain currently has no tariffs or quota barriers on trade with the other 27 EU member states and the three countries that also are parties to the EEA Agreement, i.e. Norway, Iceland and Liechtenstein (the single market). The "Hard Brexit" proposal is to abandon free trade with these 30 countries, hoping to replace this with new free trade, or nearly free-trade, agreements, both in Europe and elsewhere in the world. Since exports of goods and services to 27 of these 30 countries account for around 12.9% of Britain's GDP (the share of Britain's economy, not of its exports, see chapter 2), it should be obvious that any failure to replace free trade with identical volume and value of free trade within the single market or elsewhere, would damage Britain's economy. World trade is no longer expanding, so anything that reduces Britain's share of EU trade will give someone else an advantage. This is one reason why some EU member states would be glad to be rid of Britain; Britain's loss would be their gain.

There is a basic problem with Hard Brexit. At 12.9% of GDP, Britain's exports of goods and services to the EU exceeds the total share of GDP accounted for by British manufacturing. Only 10% of British GDP arises from all its manufacturing businesses (there may be differences in how these statistics are calculated, but the basic principle is unarguable). Given that some British manufacturing is for UK use and some for export outside the EU, a radical increase in Britain's manufacturing output would be needed plus a major increase in non-EU sales of goods in order to stand still. Why? Goods sales that are subject to tariffs, quotas and customs checks to export to Europe will inevitably be somewhat less than if Britain remained within the single market. It does not help that Hard Brexit also restricts Britain's cross-border manufacturing work, as we shall see shortly.

Services are treated differently from goods in free-trade agreements. Services sometimes need licenses which can be obtained cross-border within the EEA single market. Absent the EEA cross-border provisions, British businesses and those from the rest of the world based in Britain, have to relocate in order to provide the same services throughout the single market. This is why many banks and the Lloyds insurance market are already planning to move work away from the UK. Whereas tariffs, quotas and customs checks reduce sales of manufactured goods, services sold on cross-border passports will be lost completely. Selling more manufactured goods elsewhere in the world cannot compensate for the scale of such losses; and as explained above, the manufacturing sector would need a major renaissance.

Conversely, people residing in Britain cannot easily provide services that are regulated elsewhere in the world. If a business wants to provide banking services to most Asian countries, unless Asian residents travel to the UK to open accounts in the

UK, it needs to have a banking licence in the target country and staff on the ground. Even America, the one other big single market for goods in the world, has state by state licensing of many professional occupations.

Britain will have to renegotiate trade with the EU commission which acts on behalf of the other 27 EU member states, who negotiate as one single entity. However, it could strike separate arrangements with the EEA three, since the EEA Agreement, which binds them into the single market, will be severed on exit, unless negotiated otherwise. Because Britain is so dependent on exports to the single market, the trade arrangements with the EU 27 (and therefore also the EEA three) ought to be agreed before giving Article 50 notice. This will inevitably mean a new UK-EU agreement which will take time to negotiate. Giving notice first then hoping to negotiate against a deadline, when all power has moved to the EU, is a sure formula for wrecking existing trade. Absent an agreement with the EU, Britain would have no trade agreements on exit day. But Hard Brexit can only produce single market access with tariffs, quotas and customs checks, which will reduce British sales of goods. There will be no passporting of services, which will decimate Britain's financial services industry and its ability to work cross-border.

Hard Brexit will take Britain outside the customs union. Any future free-trade agreement, no matter how advantageous, will be limited by this, in addition to any tariffs and quotas. The situation would be like the present one with the EEA three, where Britain has free trade now but both parties have to operate customs checks. Extending reciprocal customs checks to another 27 countries that are currently major trading partners puts bureaucracy in the works where there is none today. Britain would have to check all commercial goods coming in and each of the other 27 would check commercial imports from Britain. Travellers both ways would be subject to customs controls. One of the main objectives of customs checks is to prevent back-door imports that avoid tariffs and quotas. This matters to Britain, which completes assembly of parts manufactured in other EU member states and manufactures parts that go to other EU member states for final assembly (often called the global supply chain, although it is mainly cross-EU border movement of partially finished goods). In the cases of the EEA three, they are not involved in significant global supply chains so customs checks have little impact. However, Britain has manufacturing that is integrated into cross-EU border supply chains and supply chains such as these need membership of the EU customs union in order to work effectively.

As a simple example, Ford has two factories making car engines in Britain. All their output is exported to other EU member states, where complete cars are assembled. Some of those complete cars are then imported to Britain. Ford is believed to be reviewing its options for manufacturing in Britain. Toyota and Nissan do the opposite: they manufacture parts elsewhere in the EU, import them to Britain where they are assembled into complete cars, then export some of those cars to other EU member states. No wonder the Japanese foreign ministry has asked for Britain to stay in the single market and EU customs union.

The EU will not grant Britain free trade unless Britain signs up for the four freedoms: goods, services, capital and people. Britain will not have unrestricted control of EU immigration and completely free trade, since free movement is at the heart of the free-trade area and is particularly important to achieve free trade in some services.

The argument that some non-European countries have free trade with the EU without free movement and therefore Britain should have the same is irrelevant for two reasons:

1. Britain is geographically in Europe even though it is leaving the EU.

2. Britain is a significant exporter of services to the EU via the "passport" which allows many services to be delivered cross-border without further local licences. Some non-European countries having free-trade agreements with the EU do benefit from concessions for financial services, each negotiated individually.

Hard Brexit and the non-EEA existing free trade countries
Britain has free trade with 56 other countries outside the single market as a result of EU trade agreements, that it will lose on exit day. Those 56 countries are all over the world, including Switzerland and seventeen Commonwealth countries, so Hard Brexit will hurt some Commonwealth trade.

As a non-EU member outside the EU customs union, Britain can negotiate its own free-trade agreements with the rest of the world. Although formal negotiations cannot start until after exit, discussions can be pushed almost to a conclusion beforehand. However, ratification can still take time as each country's democratic procedures have to be respected. It follows that even replacing like for like with the other 56 countries will cause some sort of disruption and job losses.

Hard Brexit and the rest of the world

The holy grail of Hard Brexit is that Britain will be able to forge new trade agreements where there are none now, particularly in Asia, the Commonwealth and North America.

Asia is far from an easy trade substitute. The British government restricts visas for teachers of Asian languages, which is not a good start. China will soon be in recession and the Bank for International Settlements has warned about its banking risks. Does Britain want its economic future to depend on a country likely to have a major recession?

India still has to implement its own internal market, instead of each state charging customs duty on trade between states. It is a high volume but low price market place which is not entirely suitable for existing British manufacturing exports. It would be unwise to rely on India at the moment.

Japan is very concerned about the risks to its significant investment in Britain, made on the basis that Japanese businesses use the UK as a bridgehead to the EU. Japan is also concerned about Britain's loss of influence caused by Brexit: the EU's embargo on arms sales to China is largely at British insistence. Spain and France (who want to sell arms to China) could change EU policy once Britain has departed. China could then use those imported arms to threaten Japan. Given that Japan only has self-defence forces and relies on America for serious military support,

Japan feels let down by Britain. This is an immediate example of the global fallout from Brexit. Brexit has given succour to American isolationism, which would add to the dangers Japan faces. Don't rely on Japan.

There may well be opportunities in Australia, Canada, New Zealand and other Commonwealth countries for new trade agreements, but these are relatively small markets compared to the single market. America is the one bright star where the opportunities are big enough and Britain might forge a new trade agreement. However, both America and Australia have made it clear that they put EU negotiations ahead of British negotiations. In the case of Australia, a new EU-Australia free-trade agreement could well come into force just as Britain leaves the EU.

The issue then becomes, can a trade agreement with America, on its own or with a few other countries, offset all the losses when British trade with Europe is reduced by tariffs, quotas and customs checks, and some services are lost completely? Will 318 million American consumers replace 458 million European ones? Will extra shipping and financing costs deter any trade with such distant countries as America, Canada, Australia and New Zealand?

The services Britain sells to Europe are unlikely to be much use in the American market. American banks reach European markets through London, not the other way round. European banks also place some of their capital market operations in London and will have to move these elsewhere in Europe. Cars made in Britain for export to Europe cannot be diverted economically to America. Britain sells small and medium cars in volume to Europe, but high-specification specialist cars to America. America may be a bonus, but it is unlikely to replace Britain's European trade and European integration.

New trade agreements take time to negotiate, as each partner government must consult its business interests and consider relevant infrastructure: for example, perishables can only be transported by air, which requires convenient airports and road access to them. When the agreements have been negotiated and ratified, new businesses may need to emerge before Britain can exploit the trade opportunities. If significant capital investment is required, or infrastructure developments are needed, then this will take many years.

This is the crucial problem with Hard Brexit. Replacing existing trading partners with different ones is a wrenching economic change. For sure, the losses will appear much earlier than the gains.

Four questions about trade

There are four major questions that need to be asked of all proposed changes to trading partners:

1. What estimated value of trade, including services, will Britain gain over 5, 10 and 15 years after exit day?

2. What estimated value of trade, including services, will Britain lose over the same time periods?

3. How long will it take to implement the new and therefore how long will Britain's economy be depressed before any improvement occurs?

4. Is there a break-even point at which the expected cumulative gain exceeds the cumulative loss? If so, how many years will it take to reach break-even?

Without figures, nobody will have a clue what they are talking about and the errors of the referendum campaign will be embellished. If Britain has wonderful new prospects that justify Hard Brexit, everyone needs to know what they are, now, before Article 50 notice is given.

The trade questions will determine the depth and duration of the coming recession. My early estimate of the damage to Britain was broadly 1% to 2% loss of GDP annually; other estimates have appeared from independent sources of around a 2% loss. The challenge for the Hard Brexiters, therefore, is to find completely new trade agreements that will more than neutralise any loss of EEA and non-EEA trade. Absent new trade agreements offering new opportunities for at least 12.9% of Britain's economy, Britain will be made permanently poorer by Hard Brexit. Even if total replacement could be achieved effective from exit day, which is unrealistic, there will be a gap of many years before the changeover is fully effective. At the very least, this has the makings of an economic depression, no matter what the ultimate prize.

Small and mid-sized companies have few revenue streams, and need to develop new services or products quietly while they keep older ones going. Disruptive change hits such businesses hardest.

At the other extreme large businesses, with major capital developments, have multiple revenue streams. Thus an oil major can develop one new oil field while earning income from many other oil fields. This is why large businesses are less exposed to Brexit. They can pick and choose what they do, knowing that their ongoing revenue streams will tide them over the disruption. The British government must be careful not to pay too much attention to large businesses; they matter, but are atypical.

Other consequences of Hard Brexit

Individuals are also considering their choices, applying for second passports where they have an entitlement to them, and contemplating emigration if they are highly skilled and attractive to countries welcoming their skills. Racism is on the rise; recession will cause more debt defaults and a further increase in poverty.

Britons living in Europe may return, but immigration of other European nationalities into Britain will decline. Britain could well finish up with two unintended consequences:

1. Emigration of the wealth creators as skilled Britons, skilled Europeans and skilled dual nationals depart to a less insular environment.

2. The return of expatriates, many of whom will be elderly and needing health care. Some may be deserting homes abroad that they cannot sell, so will need social services support (in the credit crunch homes in Spain had to be abandoned).

Britain could well have a net population increase from these trends and would certainly replace taxes paid by younger workers by extra demand for health care and support for the elderly. Because of these consequences, immigration should not be allowed to dictate strategy.

Travelling in Europe

Britons take it for granted that they can hop on a plane for a holiday, drive through the channel tunnel to go shopping, or take the train to Paris on business. With Hard Brexit, none of these will be easy. It is now politically impossible for Britain to join the Schengen zone. Britons will therefore require Schengen visas for most trips to Europe. Non-Schengen member states such as Cyprus will impose their own requirements.

The Schengen passport-free zone includes Switzerland but not the UK or Ireland; the single currency zone includes Ireland but neither the UK nor Switzerland. At present, Britons can fly from the UK to Switzerland and go through passport control and customs. Take the train from Switzerland to Germany, France, Italy or Austria and there is a customs check on the train but no passport control. Fly back to Britain now from any of those countries and there is a passport control on arrival but no customs check. This simplicity will be lost.

Britain does not have the influence to rewrite the Schengen Agreement, although it might be able to negotiate a simpler process for Britons than the present standard visa rules. Today, someone without a free-movement passport has to apply 15 days in advance, in person, for a visa at the first destination country's embassy in the country of residence (i.e. the United Kingdom).

This costs around £50 for a single trip of up to 90 days. Proof is also required of travel medical insurance, confirmed return travel booking and evidence of the ability to maintain oneself while in the Schengen zone. Unless Britain can negotiate continuance of mutual health insurance (the present European Health Insurance Card) and a waiver of proof of financial ability to maintain oneself, visiting Europe for any purpose is going to become rather tricky. Britain cannot revert to the pre-1973 arrangements for visa-free travel because they have been scrapped across Europe, rendered obsolete by free movement.

Option 2, a loose arrangement

Various political hints from the British government suggest that it is considering leaving the single market but trying to obtain its benefits without the obligation to accept free movement and perhaps without paying for the cost of running it.

Some existing EU free-trade agreements do provide for mutual recognition of other countries' regulation. Without such an agreement, negotiations for equivalence to EU rules will be needed for every business and trade sector that exports from the UK to the EEA. For example, the new Markets in Financial Instruments Directive provides for equivalence recognition, which Switzerland is planning to achieve. The idea is to do this for as much as possible of British business. Lo and behold! The single market on the sly.

A business that is outside the EEA has three alternative ways into the single market without tariffs, quotas, customs checks for goods and licensing requirements for services:

1. The business may set up an EEA branch that falls within the jurisdiction of the single market. This causes those activities and jobs that export to the EEA, to move to the branch located within the EEA, because the service must be provided, or goods manufactured, within the single market. This is no help to the United Kingdom.

2. Where equivalence rules exist, a business may rely on an official application by its government to the EU for industry sector recognition under those equivalence rules. This requires continuing renegotiation every time the rules change. Instead of the single market rules that all EEA member states have to adopt, "equivalence" means the EU bureaucracy assesses the other country's rules and procedures to ensure they are satisfactory. At present, "equivalence" is only available to parts of financial services, which means that some parts of financial services could survive in the UK. However, such survival would be subject to change and interference from the EU every time the EU made a new rule. There is no general equivalence for other services or for goods.

3. Alternatively, the government of the non-EEA country can negotiate a free-trade agreement that specifies which sectors are included. This is the situation with Singapore, which has a free-trade agreement, including most services, negotiated but awaiting ratification. This can take years to achieve: negotiations with Singapore started in 2009 and the agreement is expected to come into force in 2018 or 2019, just in time for Britain to miss out on its benefits. Whenever negotiations are needed, they can drag on for

years and be derailed by a change in market conditions that causes rule changes outside the negotiators' control.

There is no chance that the EU will allow Britain anything like its present free trade and passported services on a sufficient scale to avoid economic damage in Britain, without the obligations that go with single market membership. Credit the EU with the nous to see through the "access" claim. "Access" is a political fig-leaf to hide the paucity of what is possible. Talk of "single market access" is as meaningless as "Brexit means Brexit." Over 100 countries have "single market access" and are subject to the EU customs union common external tariff.

If anything, this is a worse option than Hard Brexit. Because of the continuing uncertainty, businesses will move elsewhere, slim down, or close completely. No rational business would hang on and hope for an equivalence agreement to descend from the heavens. And so, apart from minor distinctions in tables 1 and 2 later in this chapter, this book will treat this form of unique arrangement as a political chimera and not further distinguish it from Hard Brexit. The damage will be as bad as Hard Brexit or even worse. Certainly no improvement. The song of the sirens said "Come here"; next, the shipwreck.

Option 3, staying in the single market: "Soft Brexit" ("Brexit-lite")

In this option, Britain stays in the single market (EEA) but not in the EU. This would satisfy the referendum result, which was a vote to leave the EU, while preserving most of the trade benefits vis-a-vis Europe. Britain would keep free trade with the EU 27 plus EEA three countries. It would have some control over fisheries, but fisheries control would be constrained by the geographic realities, that British territorial waters would be adjacent to those of eight EU member states operating the common fisheries policy. Free movement means that Britons will be able to travel easily around Europe, as now, compared to the visa restrictions of Hard Brexit.

There are a number of downsides to Soft Brexit compared to Britain's present EU membership:

1. Britain would still be required to pay substantial contributions into the EU budget to meet the cost of running the single market, using the fixed formula in the EEA Agreement in lieu of the member states' periodic budget negotiations, but would not receive any rebates or subsidies.

2. Britain would be required to implement all single market directives and product specification requirements, but would no longer have any influence in formulating them.

3. Britain would still have to sign up for the four freedoms (goods, services, capital and people). This would not satisfy those who thought they were voting to take back control of immigration, but that was not part of the referendum question. It was added by the Vote Leave campaigners through the media.

However, many of the economic negatives about Hard Brexit

would fall away once it became clear that Britain was negotiating to leave the formal EU institutions but staying in the single market. In order to maintain EEA membership and implement option 3, the UK's participation in the EEA Agreement will need to be maintained. Therefore, the EEA Agreement will need to be singled out from the other treaties to be terminated on exit day, and UK participation retained, which will keep Britain in the single market and keep all the services passports in place.

This is probably the only option which should lead to Article 50 notice being given in 2017. It may also be the only option that can unite a reasonable majority of Remainers and Leavers, since it takes Britain out of the EU's institutions while preserving Britain's European trade. However, it obliges Britain to implement single-market rules made without any British input. This does not satisfy those who demand an end to free movement but, as already explained, immigration should not be allowed to dictate strategy.

There are two variations of Soft Brexit. Both involve staying in the single market. The difference is whether Britain leaves the customs union or stays within it.

Soft Brexit outside the customs union
If Britain chooses to leave the customs union, then it will be free to strike its own trade deals with the rest of the world, just like the other three EEA countries now. The existing 56 trade agreements with countries outside the single market would still be disrupted, in exactly the same way as they would be disrupted by Hard Brexit. British exports to the EU will be subject to rules of origin and paperwork to prove that tariffs and quotas are not

being circumvented, and agricultural exports to the EU will be limited by tariffs as agriculture is excluded from the EEA Agreement. Even with Soft Brexit outside the customs union, Britain needs answers to the four trade questions.

Soft Brexit inside the customs union

Staying inside the customs union means that Britain will not gain the ability to negotiate its own free-trade agreements with the rest of the world. It will continue to rely on the EU instead.

There are three important gains compared to Soft Brexit outside the customs union:

1. Britain would preserve its cross-border manufacturing work.

2. Agricultural exports to the EU will be maintained as they will not be subject to tariffs.

3. Britain's existing trade agreements with 56 non-EEA countries will be maintained.

In addition to retaining United Kingdom participation in the EEA Agreement, a new treaty will be needed as Britain would want to insist on the right to be involved in negotiating future trade agreements. This will be a little more complex than Soft Brexit outside the customs union, but simpler than either Hard Brexit or the option that is discussed next: a Close Association agreement.

Option 4: negotiating a Close Association agreement

With this option, Britain would stay in the single market and the EU customs union, and the EU would still negotiate trade with other countries. However, Britain could pick and choose which parts of non-single market European law it would implement, such as environmental law. When Britain's present prime minister was Home Secretary, Britain opted out of all measures for police, justice and home affairs, then opted back in to only those 35 measures that Britain wanted, such as the European arrest warrant. It is possible to negotiate some European law *à la carte*. Britain would have to apply single market and customs laws made by the EU, but would be free to choose which other EU laws to apply in Britain.

Britain will need the right to participate in trade negotiations and would still have to make budget contributions and lose all its rebates. Again, this satisfies the referendum result and removes the economic negatives about Hard Brexit.

A recent proposal circulated by the Bruegel think tank for a Continental Partnership to replace the EEA is somewhat similar to this concept of a unique Association agreement: in the single market, outside the formal institutions, yet able to influence relevant European law. The problem with any form of Association agreement is that it will take much more than two years to negotiate and implement. The attraction, even if Soft Brexit within the customs union has to be adopted as an interim measure, is that it is probably the only form of Brexit that will satisfy Scotland.

The World Trade Organisation

The World Trade Organisation (WTO) does not of itself provide free trade; its rules say how such agreements are to be negotiated. So when you hear politicians talking about trading under WTO rules, all you are hearing is a variation of the Canadian misunderstanding that we will learn more about in chapter 2. There is no automatic right to total free trade, without tariffs or quotas, under WTO rules. WTO rules are far from an easy solution.

Britain is currently a member of the WTO under membership terms that are common to all EU member states. These require Britain, for each separate class of goods, to either impose no duty on imports from all other WTO members or to impose a standard rate that is the same for everyone. Specific anti-dumping measures (such as for steel, see chapter 2) are therefore impossible, as is retaliation against any country imposing punitive duties. Unless and until Britain renegotiates its WTO membership, it has limited freedom to do as it likes in negotiating its own trade agreements.

Both Hard Brexit and Soft Brexit outside the EU customs union are exposed to the risk of a conflict between Britain's EU trading terms, those Britain can negotiate elsewhere, and what Britain is able to do under WTO rules. For its part, the EU also has constraints on what it can offer. WTO rules require the EU to impose its common external tariff on Britain, just as it does with any other non-EEA nation lacking a free-trade agreement: Britain either has a free-trade agreement with the EU or it does not. There is no half-way house.

Since the EU will only discuss trade within the two-year window after invoking Article 50, a complex agreement that needs ratification by every country and has to comply with both Britain's present and future WTO obligations (which may change from now) is almost impossible to achieve.

Another trade fable is that Britain can declare unilateral free trade, impose no tariffs or quotas on imports from the EU, and pass the loss to British businesses who will pay the common external tariff on their exports to the EU. Since serious consideration is already being given to forcing financial services businesses out of Britain, one can only say that this seems to be an agenda to shut down British trade. Hardly a route to prosperity. The WTO comes into this, because WTO rules demand equal treatment for all WTO members. Therefore if Britain unilaterally abolishes tariffs for all imports from the EU, it must also abolish those tariffs for the same classes of goods on imports from any WTO member anywhere in the world. No basis for future trade negotiations. Also, by its own laws, America can only negotiate free-trade agreements with countries that have WTO membership and tariff schedules in effect: another practical constraint on the dream of free-trade with America.

Evaluating the Brexit alternatives

Hard Brexit, the loose arrangement and Soft Brexit outside the customs union all involve the same disruption to 56 trade agreements with the world beyond Europe, but both variations of Soft Brexit reduce or avoid disruption to European trade. For this comparison, the Close Association agreement is identical to Soft Brexit inside the EU customs union. In a nutshell:

	Hard Brexit	**Loose arrangement**	**Soft Brexit outside EU customs union**	**Soft Brexit inside customs union**
Europe – manufacturing	Lost work	Uncertain amount of lost work	Cross-border work lost	No loss of work
Europe – services	Lost work	Uncertain amount of lost work	No loss of work	No loss of work
Europe – agriculture	Some exports lost	Some exports lost	Some exports lost	No loss of exports
Countries with existing free-trade agreements	UK needs new agreements	UK needs new agreements	UK needs new agreements	Existing free trade kept
Countries without existing free-trade agreements	UK needs new agreements	UK needs new agreements	UK needs new agreements	Agreements through EU
Overall effect	Service businesses lost, some manufacturing work and agricultural exports lost until new opportunities take effect	Some service businesses lost, some manufacturing work and agricultural exports lost until new opportunities take effect	Services kept, some manufacturing work and agricultural exports lost until new opportunities take effect	No loss of work in services / manufacturing, no loss of agricultural exports

Note: "Europe" here means the 27 other EU countries plus the three included in the EEA Agreement

Table 1: Hard versus Soft Brexit

For clarity, table 1 is available at www.sparklingbooks.com/brexit.html

If Britain is to keep its cross-border manufacturing then its choices are limited to Soft Brexit within the EU customs union or the Close Association agreement. If it is prepared to sacrifice jobs that depend on cross-EU border manufacturing and also lose some agricultural exports, then it can consider Soft Brexit outside the customs union.

For all options, Britain would give up formal membership of the EU, its place in the European council, its commissioner and its seats in the European parliament. This will satisfy the referendum question: "Should the United Kingdom remain a member of the European Union or leave the European Union?"

The arguments for Britain leaving the EU have been nationalistic (British laws for British people, end immigration) or pie-in-the-sky (tariff barriers on our European trade will not matter, we can trade with Asia instead and anyway the EU will give us free trade without any British obligations). With China heading for a recession, the Asian trade argument is as false as the belief that the EU will agree free trade, including free trade in services, with Hard Brexit.

The coming recession

Unlike the disinformation that has preceded past recessions and financial crises, this time round the establishment are working hard to ensure their excuses are ready for the next recession. The previous Chancellor, the Governor of the Bank of England and the Office for Budgetary Responsibility all issued warnings long before the referendum campaign; the present Prime Minister has added to them. Be in no doubt: the slump in commodities will be translated into a global recession. The troubles of oil, steel and retail will spread. Meanwhile, announcing a choice of any Brexit option that restricts Britain's participation in the single market will initiate Brexit-related job losses unique to Britain.

There have been a number of attempts to quantify the possible effect of leaving the EU. Within the EU, in a global recession, Britain will simply go into decline along with every other country. Britain's past destruction of manufacturing in favour of consumption, its repeated asset sales to balance the current account, its poor infrastructure, all point to an inability to withstand adverse global economic forces. Outside the EU there will be interim trade losses, which means that the British economy will perform worse than the European average. Exactly how much worse will only be discovered with the efflux of time. In chapter 2 we will look at what happened when Britain joined the common market in 1973 for clues about a reversal in strategy.

A word about capital markets

Capital markets discount the future by varying time periods. But, just as nations and their economies are interlinked, so are capital markets. The FTSE 100, in particular, largely follows Wall Street. Some politicians and tabloid newspapers have claimed that the recovery in the FTSE 100 in July to September 2016 shows that Brexit will be harmless. This is mistaken. The FTSE 100 is dominated by international businesses that will largely prosper from the drop in the pound Sterling, whereas the FTSE 250 is more representative of British businesses; it has not done well. The level of the FTSE 100 does not foretell the state of Britain when businesses decide to relocate elsewhere should the government choose Hard Brexit. In the meantime, Britons will mostly suffer from the currency's fall.

Brexit summary

The table overleaf shows key points about the main options, including the non-trade factors discussed in chapter 3. In this table, the loose arrangement is included within Hard Brexit as it is little different. For clarity, this table is also available at www.sparklingbooks.com/brexit.html

	Options 1 & 2 Hard Brexit	Option 3 Soft Brexit	Option 4 Close Association
Satisfy referendum question	Yes	Yes	Yes
Interim trade loss	Severe (a)	See note (b)	None
UK stays in single market	No	Yes	Yes
UK stays in EU customs union	No	Optional (c, f)	Yes
Impact on manufacturing	See note (d)	See note (b)	None
Impact on services	Severe (a)	None	None
Impact on agricultural exports	Some loss	See note (b)	None
Depth of next recession	Depression	See note (e)	Similar to EU
Scotland seeks independence (f)	Very likely	Possible	Unlikely
N Ireland joins Irish Republic (f)	Probable (g)	Possible (h)	Unlikely
Gibraltar joins Scotland (f)	Probable	Unlikely	No
Easy travel to 31 countries (i)	No	Yes	Yes

(a) with option 2, a few trade sectors will not be affected

(b) none if UK stays in EU customs union, some lost if UK outside EU customs union

(c) staying in EU customs union solves cross-border manufacturing and Irish border problems

(d) different product ranges needed for remote markets compared to Europe

(e) worse than EU if outside EU customs union, similar to EU if inside EU customs union

(f) the non-trade issues are discussed in chapter 3

(g) Northern Ireland customs and immigration border controls if no union with Irish Republic

(h) customs border controls if no union of the two Irelands and UK not in EU customs union

(i) including education, working, emigration, retirement and health care

Table 2: Key points about the main Brexit options

2 The importance of free trade

For two centuries, Britons have accepted the economic benefits of free trade. The lesson that free trade expands wealth for the benefit of all participants was probably derived from Britain's experience with its empire, which was an early trading bloc. The theory derives from David Ricardo's work early in the nineteenth century, which showed that when each nation exploited its own comparative advantage and a pair, or group, of nations did so mutually, then the total wealth of the participants would be more than if each nation imposed tariffs and other barriers to trade. It was this combined experience and understanding that led Britain to vote in favour of membership of the then European Economic Community (EEC) in 1975.

Now, Britain has voted to leave the EU. It seems that a fog of both misinformation and misconceptions has developed. In an attempt to disperse the fog, this chapter will investigate some trade issues in more detail and in particular:

1.   The history of how Britain's present free trade evolved.

2.   The "four freedoms" of the EU, the European Economic Area and British trade with Europe.

3.   British trade with the rest of the world.

Development of free trade

What is now known as the European Union grew from the Treaty of Rome, signed by six nations in 1957 and implemented on 1st January 1958. The founding member states were Belgium, France,

Italy, Luxembourg, Netherlands and West Germany. At that time West Germany, Britain and France were the three strongest nations in western Europe in the sense of both size and trade. Italy was a rising nation that was industrialising fast. Eastern Europe was under Soviet control. However, General de Gaulle saw Britain's interests as being contradictory to the others and blocked British membership at the outset. Of the four strong and rising nations, only Britain was excluded.

In 1960, Britain responded by founding a competing free-trade area, EFTA. The other founding members of EFTA were Austria, Denmark, Norway, Portugal, Sweden and Switzerland. Britain was by far the largest economy in EFTA. Thirteen years later, Britain left EFTA and joined the EEC. Others followed, and today EFTA consists of just four nations with a secretariat in Geneva:

Country	Population	Year joined
Switzerland	8.4 million	1960
Norway	5.1 million	1960
Iceland	330 thousand	1970 *(before Britain left)*
Liechtenstein	37 thousand	1991
Table 3: EFTA nations		

Today, EFTA has trade agreements in force with 36 countries outside Europe and is negotiating with 12 others. Individual

EFTA members have also negotiated their own trade agreements. For example, Iceland has recently negotiated a trade agreement with China, which is held up as one model of what Britain could do if it were free of the EU. However, Iceland's agreement with China is not a proper free-trade agreement, since it leaves many tariffs in place. China was allowed a five-year moratorium to implement some import duty reductions, but Iceland was not, which means it is one-sided rather than a truly reciprocal arrangement.

The EU has trade agreements in force with 56 countries outside the EEA, a free-trade area (the single market) linking all 28 EU member states and three of the four EFTA states, a customs union with three others and further trade negotiations in progress, including with Australia and Singapore. The EU-Canada agreement has also been widely offered as a model for Britain to follow, but again it is not for entirely free trade, since it leaves tariffs on some products and applies quotas to others, including Canadian agricultural exports to the EU. Agreements such as the EU-Canada agreement are more properly described as "managed trade." They do not bring all the economic benefits of free trade.

The EU-Canada agreement took seven years to negotiate and ratify, which demonstrates the possible blockages Britain may face, because every EU member state can have a veto on each and every treaty.

The four freedoms, EEA, EFTA and British trade with the EU

At the core of the various treaties giving legal effect to the EU are the "four freedoms":

1. Free movement of goods: no tariffs, no quotas and no customs checks across borders.

2. Free supply of services: passporting across borders (using a licence issued in one member state to practise in another).

3. Free movement of capital: money can move freely between member states; capital markets can function cross-border. For example, bank accounts can be opened cross-border and the Euro can be bought and sold in London even though London is outside the Euro-zone.

4. Free movement of labour and people: the right to travel, work, study, live and retire in any member state.

The first, third and fourth have been completely achieved, while work is progressing on free trade in services. Britain is strong in services and therefore would benefit from completion of the single market in services.

The European Economic Area

The EEA consists of the EU plus those three EFTA states that are party to the EEA Agreement. The EU will only grant a non-EU European country completely free trade if that country signs the EEA Agreement, which presupposes EFTA membership. Free trade between a post-Brexit Britain and the other 27 EU member states can be achieved if Britain joins EFTA and hence becomes an EFTA party to the EEA Agreement, instead of its present status as an EU party to the EEA Agreement; or if Britain's participation in the EEA Agreement is left intact at exit.

Here we need to look at what else the EEA Agreement requires apart from the four freedoms. There are two key points:

1. The non-EU member state must implement all single market directives (changes to relevant EU law) as they come into force, including applying all product specifications and regulations. The EU makes the rules and the other countries observe them. At present Britain is able to influence new EU directives and product specifications through negotiation between the bureaucracies and through the legislative process. As an example: in financial services, non-EEA firms can only do business in the UK if their customers make a "legitimate approach" at their own initiative. This is UK law, not EU law. Version 2 of the Markets in Financial Instruments Directive, coming into force in January 2018, will make "legitimate approach" legal across the entire EEA. This has come about because HM Treasury successfully argued that Britain's legitimate approach rules ought to be kept and become EU-wide. As an EEA member state outside the EU, Britain would have no such influence on new EU legislation. British interests would count for nothing.

2. The non-EU member state must contribute to the EU budget, to meet the cost of running the free-trade area. The EEA agreement also lays down that the non-EU states contribute to the EU budget in the proportion that their GDP bears to the entire EU/EEA combination. Unlike

Britain's usual budget negotiations as an EU member state, there is no influence: you just pay for membership of the free-trade area. Norway, Iceland and Liechtenstein all implement the four freedoms and pay into the EU budget. Switzerland also pays into the EU budget in exchange for its bilateral trade treaties.

The four freedoms apply to all the 28 EU member states (including, at present, the United Kingdom). They also apply to three of the four EFTA members, through the EEA Agreement which links Norway, Iceland and Liechtenstein into the single market. Britons are free to travel and emigrate to any of those countries and also to Switzerland.

Switzerland is not a party to the EEA Agreement, but achieves free trade in many goods via bilateral treaties with the EU. It is a party by treaty to free movement of labour and people. Despite being an EFTA member, Switzerland opted out of the EEA Agreement and therefore is not a party to free supply of services and free movement of capital (although it has no restrictions on capital flows for managed investment services). The unusual position of Switzerland arises from it being a past candidate country for EU membership. Candidate countries whose membership application stalls, usually keep what they have already negotiated.

Joining EFTA

One option is for Britain to join EFTA. By coincidence, the EFTA summer ministerial meeting was on 27th June 2016, and it resulted in this statement: "The EFTA Ministers discussed the outcome of the United Kingdom's referendum on the European Union and its possible implications. They underlined the importance of maintaining close trade relations with the United Kingdom, which is one of the major trading partners of the EFTA countries."

The statement does not say "Welcome back to EFTA, Britain" because it is not clear that all four EFTA members would wish Britain to rejoin. EFTA would certainly have more clout with Britain as a member, but each existing member of EFTA has a veto. Britain has no automatic right to join EFTA and may be unwelcome given how Britain jilted EFTA in 1973 and bullied Iceland (using anti-terrorism legislation to nationalise Icelandic bank assets in the UK) in 2008. Some Britons will also remember the cod wars with Iceland. Britain cannot presume that it will be welcome. Norway has already said that it does not want a large country such as Britain destabilising EFTA. Planning on the basis of joining EFTA would be risky. Even if EFTA should roll out the red carpet, Britain would still have less free trade with the rest of the world, because (even including Britain) EFTA is far smaller than the EU and, as noted, has fewer free-trade agreements with the rest of the world.

Free trade or migration?
To continue to trade freely with the EU, then, Britain could join EFTA or stay as a non-EFTA party to the EEA Agreement (both of which need separate negotiation). It would continue to pay into the EU budget and continue to allow free movement of people. This is the point at which trade and politics start to get

mixed up, because Vote Leave had these statements on its website:

1. "We should negotiate a new UK-EU deal based on free trade and friendly co-operation." Along with free trade, free movement of capital and passported services would also be lost should Britain fail to maintain the four freedoms. This would have a devastating effect on financial markets and the City.

2. "We regain legal control of migration." Because any UK-EU free trade deal will require Britain to continue with the four freedoms, it can be seen that taking control of Britain's borders is incompatible with completely free trade. Britain can have free trade but no change in the rights of EU and EFTA citizens to reside and work in Britain; or it can control its borders, but lose free trade.

3. "We stop sending £350 million every week to Brussels." This can only be achieved if Britain leaves the single market, since all single-market participants share the cost of running it.

There is little chance that any future exit negotiations will change the contradiction between free trade and free movement. Why should the EU give up cherished principles for Britain's benefit? The same argument applies to budget contributions. Why should the EU let Britain keep free trade without paying its share of the costs of running the free-trade area? But this brings us to the claim that Britain can spend less on the EU. At the moment, Britain gets regional support through a grant system which is only available to EU member states. Scotland, Wales, Northern Ireland and Cornwall all benefit from EU regional support. Britain's farmers get EU industry support: the average farming income is about £20,000, of which just over half is EU support. On the other hand, EEA members get no EU financial support. So in leaving the EU, Britain will lose its EU support but still pay budget contributions if it stays in the single market.

Alternative trading relationships with the EU
The significant trading relationships were discussed in chapter 1. Other possible trading relationships with the EU were put forward as the basis for providing free trade without budget contributions and without free movement of people. We need to understand them. They are:

1. The customs union allows goods to move without checks, tariffs or quotas. Andorra, San Marino and Turkey have a customs union with the EU but control their own borders. For the first two, this is a practical necessity, since they are tiny states embedded between or within EU members. Turkey was granted a partial customs union twenty years ago as part of its candidate status for EU membership. In all three cases, the relevant agreements set out arrangements unique to the circumstances of each state. Britain is neither a tiny state embedded between or within other EU members, nor will it be a candidate for EU membership, so this option does not obviously fit as a stand-alone solution. Will the EU even contemplate allowing the UK to stay in the customs union but outside

the single market? Being in the customs union, however, does fit as an option with Soft Brexit or as part of the Close Association agreement.

2. Albania, Bosnia, Serbia and Ukraine. Albania, Bosnia and Serbia are candidate states for EU membership, while Ukraine is being offered a stabilisation process. Britain would hardly fit these categories. However, the adoption of the Albanian model by Vote Leave as a proposed solution to the contradictions between trade, budget contributions and immigration, does say something about Britain's role in the world.

Talk of sovereignty by Hard Brexiters amounts to the sovereignty of the desert island castaway. An empty shell. Isolation. Outside the EU, Britain would be somewhere between such a desert island castaway with meaningless sovereignty and having insignificant influence in the world. Sovereignty is constrained in many ways: for example, international treaties restrict the powers of government; markets and natural resources impose practical constraints. The real purpose of the demand to reclaim sovereignty is to allow government much more freedom from external constraints, giving the authorities more power to do as they like.

On 30th March 2016, *The Independent* reported the chief executive of Vote Leave saying the UK would be able to secure a post-Brexit trade deal that would enable economic growth and job creation, adding that "the biggest risk to the UK economy… is Britain remaining in a declining political union where we are outvoted and our trade is held back." There are no less than three mistakes implicit in this statement:

1. That Britain will get a better trade deal with the EU than it has now is impossible, since there are currently no tariff, quota or customs barriers. Chapter 1 shows the opposite, that a worse deal is likely, which will cause economic damage and job losses.

2. That Britain will do better on its own is beyond parody as a fantasy.

3. In my view, the statement "Our trade is held back by the EU" is a travesty of the truth. The EU has been instrumental in Britain expanding its trade with the rest of the world through 56 agreements with other countries, and more are under negotiation.

The EU trade contradiction is simple. Free trade with the EU cannot be achieved together with border control, budget savings and regaining sovereignty.

While examining contradictions, let's look into the problems of British steel, which are omissions of inconvenient facts:

1. Either Britain allows free trade in steel, or it subsidises steel. It cannot do both. China, for example, would never agree any trade deal if it was blocked from selling its surplus steel in Britain.

2. Over half the output of British steel is exported to the EU. Hard Brexit would make it more difficult for British steel

to compete in its largest market.

3. If (outside the single market) the UK government tries to subsidise steel in Britain, it will need a pocket as deep and long as China's or Germany's. Britain does not have the spare taxation revenues to outbid larger countries in a subsidy war.

4. Does Britain want cheaper prices, for example of cars, or higher prices via tariffs and subsidies? Britain cannot have both.

5. In 2014, the EU proposed a higher external tariff on steel to protect against Chinese dumping, but Britain, along with some other members, *blocked* the proposal.

Britain needs the single market but the EU does not need Britain

At present 44% of Britain's exports go to the EU and 53% of its imports come from the EU. These figures imply that Britain runs a trade deficit with the EU. One frequently heard argument is that the EU needs Britain because of those 53% British imports. The implicit suggestion is that 27 EU member states each send 53% of their exports to the UK. However, 53% is an aggregate from 27 member states, and for each of those 27 member states, it is their individual exports to Britain that matter to them.

Exports from those 27 EU member states to the UK vary. The largest exporter to the UK, in percentage terms of its total exports, is the Irish Republic, which for reasons of geography, history and language, sends 15% of its exports (note, not 15% of its GDP) to Britain. Germany is a major exporter to the UK, thanks to British fondness for Mercedes, BMW and Audi cars, but Germany's exports to the UK are less than 8% of its total exports (not 8% of its GDP). The average EU member state exports only 3.1% of GDP to Britain, whereas Britain exports 12.9% of its GDP to the 27 other member states. Leaving the EU would hurt Britain and Ireland, but be of little impact elsewhere. Given that those Mercedes, BMW and Audi cars are frequently bought by people working in financial services, Hard Brexit would send some of those jobs elsewhere. Germany would then make its sales of premium cars elsewhere in the EU instead of in Britain. Germany's need for Britain would be even less than now.

Rotterdam effect

Another factor in measuring trade between Britain and the EU is that both imports to Britain and exports from Britain are sometimes routed through other EU member states, from and to countries outside the EU. This particularly occurs when goods are imported in bulk from a non-EU country into an EU port then re-documented and trans-shipped between that port and several EU member states, including Britain. It is commonly described as the "Rotterdam effect" because Rotterdam is the largest such port providing bulk trans-shipment facilities; Antwerp and Genoa provide similar facilities. It can also happen in reverse to exports, but seems to mainly affect imports.

Where such imports to Britain are re-documented when trans-shipped, they will show incorrectly as British imports from the EU instead of from outside the EU. Nobody has precise figures for this, but Britain's trade with the Netherlands probably includes manufactured goods that are wrongly counted as

imports from within the EU even though they originated
elsewhere. Britain's apparent trade deficit with the EU may be a
non-existent artifice of inadequate statistics. A paper by the
Office for National Statistics in the national archives suggests that
Britain's true imports from the EU and exports to the EU,
excluding trans-shipped goods that originate outside the EU,
may be roughly in balance.

Another way of analysing trade between Britain and the EU is
to relate it to GDP, that is as a proportion of economic activity.
Here are the figures:

Britain's exports to the EU	12.9% of British GDP
Ireland's exports to Britain	11.5% of Irish GDP
Dutch exports to Britain	7.2% of Dutch GDP
EU average exports to Britain	3.1% of each member state's GDP

Table 4: EU trade in relation to GDP

The Netherlands is high on this list because of the Rotterdam
effect. Britain is far more dependent on exports to the EU than
the other 27 EU members are dependent on exports to Britain. In
short, apart from Ireland, the EU does not need Britain. There is
no justification for the claim that the EU needs Britain. Britain's
exports to the EU are four times the average EU member state's
exports to Britain, measured as a share of each member state's

national GDP. The shares of GDP accounted for by national exports demonstrate the exact opposite, that Britain needs the EU. The Brexit trade risks have been badly misunderstood. The UK also has a high share of inward investment into the EU from elsewhere in the world, notably Japan; this and Britain's strength in services explain why Britain is so dependent on exports to the EU.

Hard Brexit will cause some UK employers to move elsewhere. The City will lose work to Paris and Frankfurt, with inevitable tax losses for the government and hence further austerity. Some foreign manufacturers based in the UK and exporting to EU markets will decamp. Jobs will be lost as trade declines.

The EU has a common external tariff which all member states apply to imports from countries outside the EU that do not have trade agreements. The tariff varies. Its weighted average is 6.7% of declared value of goods, but it is 18% on agricultural products. Britain's farmers will be hit on two or even three fronts by Hard Brexit: 18% tariffs on exports to the EU; loss of EU farming subsidies; and in the poorer regions of Britain, loss of regional aid. The Treasury promise to pay EU regional aid, if Britain leaves the EU before 2020, but will pay this only until 2020. The value of this is trivial because of the short time span.

Economic impact of leaving the single market
There have been attempts to estimate the economic impact of leaving the EU and single market via Hard Brexit. An estimate can be derived from what happened when Britain joined. British exports rose by about 7% in the first few years following

membership in 1973.

Subsequent completion of the single market for goods caused a further 9% rise in British exports to the EU. Leaving and going-it-alone will reverse the gains Britain achieved. If all 12.9% of Britain's GDP (its exports to the EU of both goods and services) shrinks by, say, 15%, then assuming services behave the same way as goods, total GDP would fall by 1.9%. But since some services need licences (the passport) they cannot be provided from outside the single market, which means GDP will shrink by more than this, affecting jobs and provoking a recession. A multiplier effect will then spread the damage: those whose work is affected will spend less, causing other businesses to fail and Britons to lose work. Leaving the single market could well cost the British economy 5% of GDP, as much as the share of population accounted for by EU nationals resident in Britain.

The EEC in 1973 consisted of just nine member states after Britain joined. The twin effects of 7% growth in British exports post-accession and 9% subsequently were therefore achieved in a single market of just nine countries. Now Britain is leaving a single market of 31 countries, three and a half times the size of the common market as it stood in 1973. It follows that the loss of trade by reversing the process will be much more than the gains in trade after accession, another warning about the perils of Hard Brexit.

Trade with the rest of the world

Britain's trade with the non-EU world is growing faster than its EU trade because the EU has been successful in bringing more trade deals with other countries into effect. About two-thirds of the EU's trade agreements have been signed in the last 15 years. No wonder British trade outside the EEA is now growing. However, it is still relatively small compared with Britain's single market trade.

Here there are three other practical issues. One is that Britain has few experienced trade negotiators of its own. Britain has been under contributing personnel to Brussels for many years, so there are few reserves to repatriate. Acquiring expertise in trade negotiations takes years. Paradoxically, Britain may need to employ foreigners to negotiate its future trade agreements.

The second is that the world has split into multiple trading blocs that negotiate with one another. Wherever you look, there are trade groups: EU, EFTA, NAFTA, Caricom, Central America, South African customs union, Mercosur, Asean. Only unloved dictatorships go it alone.

The third practical issue is that trade negotiations take time. Canada needed over five years to negotiate its trade agreement with the EU, which is still not in force. Since every EU member state has to ratify any EU agreement unless an accelerated procedure is agreed, ratification can take two to three years. Similar time scales will affect other negotiations, including any new agreements with countries such as America and China. It is likely that, outside the EU and its customs union and outside EFTA, Britain could achieve no more than a handful of trade agreements with the rest of the world in the next ten years. Possibly nowhere near enough to replace its present trade agreements that come with EU membership, and certainly not enough to replace lost work in services if Britain leaves the single market.

3 A British view of non-trade factors

"Fog in channel, continent isolated"

This newspaper headline from the 1930s neatly summarises British attitudes to Europe. For most of the seventeenth, eighteenth and nineteenth centuries, British policy was built around preventing a strong European power from emerging. Post-1945, linking European states in an arrangement for shared sovereignty continued that policy and reduced the inclination of others to resort to force of arms to settle disputes.

Non-trade factors therefore affect Britain's choice, in addition to the economic factors relating to trade. But given the potential damage that Hard Brexit would cause to Britain, deciding what to do is not just a matter for politicians and civil servants. All factual research done by the civil service should be published. Only a truly open government can prevent the disconnection between people and parliament widening.

The important factors other than trade that will need to be evaluated in deciding which Brexit option to choose are:

1. Keeping the United Kingdom together.

2. Reconciliation between the different groups of Britons to bring national unity in place of the deep divisions that were exposed by the referendum.

3. British citizens living within free-movement countries.

4. The risk of political upsets.

5. Inequality and austerity.

6. Regulation.

7. Negotiating with the EU.

Keeping the United Kingdom together

The critical problem here is Scotland, which does not wish to leave the EU. The Scots understand that immigration and an expanding economy go hand-in-hand.

The Scottish First Minister has set out her negotiating position, demanding that Scotland's wishes be respected, which are:

1. Continued free movement.

2. Remaining in the single market.

3. Continuing with EU support to Scottish farming and universities.

4. Keeping social protection of workers' rights and human rights.

5. A common approach to the common good, for example tackling terrorism and climate change.

6. Being able to influence single market rules.

Here is how these points relate to the various Brexit options:

What Scotland wants	Which option could satisfy this?
Continued free movement	Both variations of Soft Brexit, and the Close Association agreement
Remaining in the single market	Both variations of Soft Brexit, and the Close Association agreement
Continuing with EU support to Scottish farming and universities	None, because any form of Brexit will lose EU support. Scotland may demand later that England reimburse its losses
Keeping social protection of workers' rights and human rights	None, although workers' rights could be negotiated in a Close Association agreement, or transferred to UK law. The UK government has undertaken to transfer workers' rights to UK law. Human rights are governed by a separate European convention
A common approach to the common good, for example tackling terrorism and climate change	Close Association agreement
Being able to influence single market rules	Close Association agreement

Table 5: Satisfying Scotland

Hard Brexit does nothing for Scotland. Most of the points can be satisfied by a Close Association, but even Soft Brexit only satisfies two points.

There are three contrary factors that may keep Scotland in the United Kingdom. They are:

1. The Scottish First Minister will not wish to risk another referendum unless she is sure to win. Both Hard Brexit and Soft Brexit outside the customs union will improve her chances in the proposed second independence referendum.

2. Falling oil prices make Scottish independence economics a little shaky, even with the lower pound Sterling, but Scotland could offer banks an alternative to Frankfurt.

3. About 29% of Scotland's GDP is sold to the rest of the United Kingdom, so tariff barriers resulting from Scottish independence may hurt Scotland.

The United Kingdom parliament has given up its right to legislate in respect of matters devolved to Scotland, and the Scotland Act 1998 prevents the Scottish parliament from making any legislation contrary to EU law. The Scottish parliament could therefore refuse to end the primacy of EU law in Scotland. Stand by for an almighty row.

Should Scotland choose independence following Hard Brexit and stay in the EU, then the England/Scotland border would become a customs border and also an immigration border, in both directions. Border crossing would only be possible at fixed points. Delays and queues would be normal: even trains would stop for customs and passport checks. If Scotland chooses to join Schengen, visas would be needed.

The Scotland/England border problem arises if an independent Scotland stays in the EU while England is outside the EU customs union. If England were to be inside the customs union and therefore also a free-movement country there would be no border problem. If England should be outside the customs union but in the single market, there would be customs checks but no passport checks at the border.

There is currently an open border between Northern Ireland and the Irish Republic, since both countries are EU members and have a joint derogation from border control rules applicable to countries outside the Schengen area. If the UK leaves the EU choosing Hard Brexit, then the Irish border will also become an EU external border. With Soft Brexit outside the customs union, customs checks would be needed on the Irish border, just as between England and Scotland.

The EU law that permits both countries to operate a common travel area (Protocol 20 of the Treaty on the Functioning of the European Union) will no longer apply as the UK will no longer be a party to it. It is inconceivable that the EU will allow a member state, Ireland, to create a hole in the EU border by permitting a new arrangement with a non-EU country outside the customs union, since this would create a route to bypass customs controls.

The Irish Republic joined the EEC with Britain in 1973; this is what allowed the existing common travel area to continue then. To continue the common travel area now, the Irish Republic would also need to leave the EU at the same time as Britain. Politicians claiming that the common travel area can be continued are mistaken. A hard border in Ireland would be a retrograde step, as the Good Friday agreement that brought peace to Northern Ireland assumed both sides of the border would be in the EU. In order to be certain that the present border arrangements can continue, Britain would have to stay within the customs union.

Two different viewpoints have emerged in Northern Ireland. The Democratic Unionist Party, who lead the Stormont government, accept the majority UK decision to leave. However, Sinn Fein see this as an opportunity for Northern Ireland to leave the United Kingdom and reunite with the Irish Republic. As with Scotland, there is a devolution law conflict in Northern Ireland. This is being tested in the Northern Irish courts in one of two legal actions against the UK government.

There is also a risk that some of the Celtic nations make common cause against an England determined to go into isolation. Scotland could break away before exit and claim to be the successor state to the UK, without ever leaving the EU. In any break-up of the UK, Gibraltar would almost certainly join with Scotland.

Scottish independence is now a serious risk to the United Kingdom. If the SNP win independence for Scotland, Scotland could then attract businesses from England, which would see the former fraternal nations competing with one another. Another outcome might include the nuclear deterrent base being thrown out of Scotland.

What about Wales? Despite the emergence of UKIP in parts of Wales and a majority for leaving the EU, Plaid Cymru are for the EU. The First Minister in the devolved Labour government in Wales has warned that the Welsh economy will suffer severely from Brexit, because Wales is so dependent on regional support from the EU.

Anything from losing Scotland to the outcome of a complete split of multiple nations from England would be Britain's worst diplomatic and constitutional disaster ever, further diminishing British influence in the world.

Reconciling the different groups of British attitudes to Europe

Because nobody knew just what "Leave" meant, there are four different British attitudes to Europe:

1. "Remainers" – those who saw Britain's future as a major European power having influence through the EU.

2. "Anti-integrationists" – those who want to stay in the single market but eschew any involvement in EU institutions or EU law (chapter 1, options 3 or 4).

3. "Soft Brexiters" – those who believed they could stay in the single market but control immigration, contrary to the single market principle of free movement, and also those who really did not understand the issues but chose to cast a protest vote (chapter 1, option 3).

4. "Hard Brexiters" – those who want to leave the single market completely, notably the extreme right wing of Conservative MPs, a larger proportion of Conservative party members, and UKIP (chapter 1, options 1 or 2).

There were no reliable figures for the three groups of Leavers, probably because nobody said clearly what the options were.

Remainers were 48% of those who voted. The 52% was split between three other groups, all having their own ideas of what Leave meant. Many of those who voted Leave were probably either Anti-integrationists or Soft Brexiters, rather than Hard Brexiters. The three Leave groups were wildly different. Therefore a solution that appeals only to one of those groups (for example, Hard Brexit) would cause the other two groups plus the 48% of Remainers to be dissatisfied. The conflicts brought to the surface by the 23rd June 2016 referendum will only deepen as the contradictions unfold.

Given proper information, these groups might align differently. But absent a much stronger majority for a specific option, the solution does not lie within the power of British politicians. Why? Because they allowed fear of immigration to dominate the issues. Chapter 1 shows why immigration should not be allowed to determine strategy. If Britain is to avoid further tensions between the various groups of Britons, immigration must be sidelined as a Brexit issue.

British citizens residing in other free-movement countries

According to a recent House of Commons briefing paper (SN06077, 25th February 2016), 2.9 million EU citizens live in Britain, mostly working and thereby supporting public services through their taxes. 1.8 million British citizens live elsewhere in the EU, with a higher proportion of retired Britons in the sunnier climes. Another 400,000 British citizens divide their time between Britain and the rest of the EU, bringing the total of British citizens residing in the EU to 2.2 million. EFTA citizens in Britain and Britons residing in EFTA countries are excluded from these statistics.

There are reported to be over 300,000 net immigrants to Britain annually, with around half of these from the free-movement countries. In 2007, *Prospect* published an article drawing attention to the shortcomings of emigration counts (issue 140, November 2007). Flow counts are not accurate. 2.2 million British citizens live in the EU and 2.9 million EU citizens live in the UK, a difference of 700,000. These figures imply that less than five years' net immigration from the EU to Britain (150,000) accounts for the entire difference. Although EU immigration speeded up after the accession of new countries in 2007, these figures do not make complete sense and may possibly be overstating immigration.

Any right for British citizens to remain in a free-movement country after Hard Brexit may not include the right to have pension increases and the right to health care whereby their country of origin pays for retired people's health care. Existing pensions will be damaged by the decline in the pound Sterling caused by Brexit. These factors alone could drive retired Britons back to the UK with little flow in the reverse direction, adding to the strains already evident in the NHS, housing and social support.

The future of Britons living elsewhere in the other 31 free-movement countries (that is, the EU 27, plus the EEA three and Switzerland), has been confused with acquired rights under the Vienna Convention. The Vienna Convention is a UN treaty binding all signatories to norms of good behaviour in interstate relations expressed through treaties. It has no direct relevance to individuals, and does not apply in France, Norway and Iceland because these countries have chosen not to ratify it. Prior to Brexit, some Britons will have resided in one of the other 31 countries long enough to acquire the right to permanent residence under existing EU law. In other cases, Britons may seek a second nationality. But absent any satisfactory arrangement emerging from Brexit negotiations, those who have emigrated relatively recently may lose their residence rights and be forced back to Blighty.

The risk of political upsets

The risk of triggering the break-up of the United Kingdom is bad enough. What, though, would be the effect elsewhere? There are minority anti-EU parties all over Europe. The British vote to leave has given succour to them. And the end of free movement would give Spain an easy weapon to blockade Gibraltar, since Gibraltar's economy depends on a daily inflow of cross-border workers.

There are underlying nationalist contradictions of free trade versus protectionism and immigration versus economic decline. In France, these same contradictions have led to the emergence of a new political movement, "En Marche!" **The equivalent political challenge in Britain is to reconcile as many individuals as possible from the different groups of Britons so that a larger majority support the chosen option.**

The British government has a difficult task to get anything related to Brexit through the House of Commons. About 450 MPs campaigned for Remain, although some may have since changed their minds. Apart from some ten Labour MPs and one UKIP MP, the Brexiters are all in the governing Conservative party, with about 30 demanding Hard Brexit. The House of Lords is also pro-EU.

What will happen when the government tries to take legislation through the UK Parliament giving effect to the referendum result? The government's small majority could be wiped out by a pro-EU or pro-single market backbench rebellion. A confrontation with the Lords would need use of the provisions of the Parliament Act 1911 and a year's delay. But if the Commons opts for the single market, Hard Brexiters would rebel and the Conservative party could split.

Given a free vote, the Commons would either keep Britain in the single market or seek a close association agreement. If there is any further referendum it ought to be about the Brexit option choices so that it can both precede giving notice and, hopefully, provide the stage for a compromise that can be widely accepted. It cannot simply rerun the previous referendum as that would look like the establishment dictating to the people.

There has been talk of using the Royal prerogative to give notice to leave the EU without involving Parliament. This would overturn the two principles that sovereignty is the Crown in Parliament and that referendums are only advisory. In addition to the Irish case mentioned earlier, an English legal action against the UK government seeks to prevent the Royal prerogative being used. The paradox is that the undemocratic Royal prerogative would be used to enforce the will of an uninformed small numerical majority against the elected representatives of the people. This would indeed be the establishment dictating to the people. What will happen to parliamentary sovereignty?

Politics of inequality and austerity

This takes us into wider issues that have, albeit indirectly, influenced the leave/remain debate. What do the right wing in England (UKIP, some Conservative constituency activists, the tabloid press), the Front Nationale in France, and American isolationists have in common? They all appeal to the lower middle classes who once had steady well-paid work in factories or services, but are now finding their job opportunities curtailed or vanishing.

Three factors have combined to influence people. They are:

- globalisation,

- elimination of intermediary businesses such as travel agents and estate agents by the Internet, and

- financial repression by the authorities through excessive debt creation.

Ordinary people living on the poverty line are the hapless victims of these changes. Politicians in several countries have tapped into this seam of discontent, albeit each with added local factors. Those local factors include:

- political gridlock in America,

- the failure of the French socialist model, and

- policies that favour the well-off in Britain.

Britain's immigration problem is badly expressed when looked at from the effect on housing, schools and demand for health care. Immigrants are mainly younger workers. Without them, Britain would lack the ability to adequately staff its NHS and care services, and would have insufficient tax revenues to support its ageing population and pay for its real growth business: self-inflicted bureaucratic overheads!

All that has been achieved by policies of credit expansion, added to the long-term structural failings of the British economy, is an increase in inequality. The social damage will now lead to political upsets, of which Brexit is one example. The divisions in the Labour party are another example.

It is widely believed that immigration was the major factor in encouraging people to vote for Britain to leave the EU. The slogan "Take back control" was repeated constantly to great effect. However, anyone paying attention to public comments in the media would also have noted that immigration was blamed for long waiting times for doctors' and hospital appointments, and for lack of places in local schools. If a European immigrant population of barely 5% of the total population can cause such damage, then either Britain's NHS and schools must be in a much worse state than appears, or there is some other factor for dissatisfaction with them. Although the connection is unproven, the Fabian Society has demonstrated a relationship between low funding levels and high votes to leave the EU.

Health and education are not EU responsibilities. National governments of member states determine their health care and education systems; the EU has no interest in them. In the UK, they are devolved to the Scottish parliament, Welsh assembly and Stormont. That leaves England, for which the Westminster parliament acts as an *English* parliament, passing legislation that is restricted to England.

In 2007, before the credit crunch, Britain's GDP per person was £1,553 bn. The population was 61.2 million and the Retail Prices Index (RPI, a measure of price level changes) was 203.2 (at year end). Five years later, in 2012, GDP was £1,505 bn, the population was 63.7 million and the RPI was 231.5. We can calculate GDP per person at 2007 prices from these figures:

	2007	2012
Gross Domestic Product	£1,553 bn in 2007	£1,505 bn in 2012
Population	61.2 m	63.7 m
Retail Prices Index	203.2	231.5
GDP/person at that year's prices	£25,380	£23,630
GDP/person at 2007 prices	£25,380	£20,740 (23,630 x 203.2 / 231.5)

Table 6: The fall in UK living standards 2007-2012

In five years, British living standards fell by 18.3%. In addition to this fall in living standards, the UK government imposed a serious austerity programme, in which services were cut, benefits were cut, and public facilities such as health care and education were rationed by queue. The poor were particularly hard hit by austerity, with measures such as the bedroom tax, fitness for work assessments that paid scant regard to personal health and disabilities, and cuts to further education and libraries that restricted opportunities. The public comments about waiting for health appointments and lack of places in schools reflect the result of austerity. Immigration has taken the blame in public, but austerity is the real culprit. Some people are confused about where decisions come from, and the EU was a target for their anger. This is another reason why immigration must not be allowed to determine Brexit strategy.

Regulation

Politicians who favour Hard Brexit frequently cite excessive EU regulation as an impediment to Britain, and imply that there will be less bureaucratic interference outside the EU.

To understand what this is really about, we need to again examine an example of financial services regulation. Until 2007, cross-border EU/EEA financial services were governed by the Investment Services Directive, which provided a limited mutual recognition procedure between countries. As is its normal practice unless expressly prohibited, Britain gold-plated the original ISD rules – some of its then regulators increased capital requirements for financial services businesses. In 2001, when Britain merged all its financial regulators into one, the result was that identical business activities were subject to different rules according to who their previous regulator was. Britain's then-new unitary regulator, the Financial Services Authority (FSA, which has since been abolished), proposed a single comprehensive set of rules, published as Consultation Paper 97. That paper included some 600 pages of rules and guidance. The level of detail and control was excessive.

Soon after publication, FSA realised that the EU planned to replace the Investment Services Directive and therefore shelved its proposals. In 2007 the Markets in Financial Instruments Directive (MiFID) came into force, followed a few months later by the Capital Requirements Directive (CRD). It should be no surprise that CRD was copied almost verbatim from the earlier draft FSA rules. The British bureaucracy had done a grand job of providing its input to the EU. **Britain's regulatory problem is home grown.** Another misconception about the EU.

Another view about Britain's regulatory problem can be found in a paper published by a group of lawyers: "Lawyers in for Britain." The 230-odd signatories included academics and senior lawyers. They made the point that Britain outside the EU would be exposed to more regulation, as the constraints of EU membership would be gone and the British bureaucracy would be free to do as it likes. The chances are that regulation will get worse when EU law no longer applies.

Negotiating with the EU

Cheery politicians told voters that Britain would negotiate favourable exit terms, so let's look at the steps that need to be taken.

The British government has to notify the EU that the UK intends to leave. Under Article 50 of the Lisbon treaty, the remaining members then decide what terms to offer the departing member state. The departing member state has no right to participate in these discussions. Negotiation of exit terms is not under Britain's control.

Consider the point of view of the other 27, or at least the major players: Germany, France, Italy and perhaps Poland and Spain. As a result of the previous prime minister's initiative, the club of

28 has already offered its difficult member state, who does not wish to play by club rules, extra favours. There is no desire to allow this exiting member state to set any precedents. Therefore, the terms will be brutal. Take it or leave it, without concessions. British exceptionalism, the frequent demands for more from a club of equals, is another reason why some will be glad to see the back of Britain.

The Lisbon treaty also provides that if no earlier exit has been agreed, the departing member state ceases to be a member state two years after notifying the EU of its intention to leave. Only the other 27 member states have power to extend the two-year period. The EU have a number of voices in all this: commission, parliament and political leaders will all want their say. However, even if negotiations are incomplete after two years, the guillotine descends and all EU treaties then fall away. No regional grants and subsidies. No free trade with the EU, the three EEA countries and the 56 other countries Britain already has free trade with through its EU membership, and no free movement.

Western and Eastern European EU member states share their determination not to sacrifice free movement. Nonetheless, there are anti-immigration insurgencies in France, Netherlands, Germany, Sweden and Hungary, which is another reason why the EU will not give Britain any concessions. Their need is for the EU to discourage any other exit movements that might weaken itself further.

Britain has particularly annoyed eight EU members, those that, like Britain, do not use the Euro as their currency. As part of the proposed changes to Britain's membership terms, Britain's former Prime Minister negotiated an agreement that the Euro-zone majority would not impose its will on the non-Euro member states, which the other eight welcomed. The system of qualified majority voting in the European council left the non-Euro member states vulnerable to a Euro-zone majority. The Brexit vote has killed off that agreement, which was designed for Britain but just happened to benefit those eight member states as well. Brexit has therefore upset Bulgaria, Croatia, Czech Republic, Denmark, Hungary, Poland, Romania and Sweden. Not a good start to complex negotiations.

Since the EU are adamant that they will give Britain no concessions and Britain is in a weaker negotiating position than its politicians appear to recognise, only some variation of Soft Brexit, continuing the United Kingdom's single market membership, can avoid Britain creating an economic and political disaster for itself.

4 Britain and Europe

The EU is not perfect

There is some tension within the EU:

1. There is a continuing divide between those who desire more European integration and those who would prefer to draw back.

2. The single currency, the Euro, is an artificial construct that may not last.

3. Right wing insurgencies against immigration are gaining support in several member states.

Britain's uneasy relationship with Europe reflects these anxieties. This chapter considers the structure and faults of the EU and also how Britain has mishandled Europe. The Euro is discussed separately in my book *The Greatest Crash: How contradictory policies are sinking the global economy.*

What does the EU do?

In the original form of the EU, six countries agreed to pool sovereignty in a structure designed to ensure no one country could be supreme. Those founding members wanted to ensure that Europe could never again be riven by war. Free trade was at the heart of the EU, as was the right of citizens to live and work anywhere within the EU.

Although implementation has been slow and patchy, the EU

has grown into a large free-trade area, significantly larger than that of the United States of America. Britain has historically welcomed free trade and this was the rationale for the 1975 referendum.

The EU has a small number of policy areas that it exercises in superiority to all members. The main ones are trade, some commercial policy, competition policy, such legislation as is necessary to support international agreements, fisheries and monetary policy. Monetary policy only applies to the Euro-zone member states. Apart from monetary policy and fisheries, all the rest are needed to enable the single market to function.

Everything else that the EU does is in agreement with its members. It does set standards in many areas, and a genuine worry is that Britain outside the EU may well adopt less rigorous standards; as an example, for the environment. But all EU law is made in conjunction with the members, with both the European council (which represents all governments of the EU member states) and the European parliament having a say.

Because competition is an EU responsibility, the EU has the ability through its sheer size to stand up to global businesses. Such businesses can dwarf the size of national governments. Britain alone could not extract taxes from Google, but the EU has the strength to extract taxes from Apple.

Structure of the EU

The political and managerial structure of the EU is:

- a series of treaties between sovereign states;

- the European commission in Brussels, headed by appointed commissioners (the bureaucracy);

- the European council (representatives of elected ministers from national governments);

- the European parliament;

- the European Central Bank (for the Euro-zone member states only);

- the European court.

Legislation is proposed and drafted by the European commission, haggled over in the European council, tweaked by the parliament and implemented as directives enforced through the European court, which instruct member states to incorporate their terms into domestic law. In reality, the European council is more like a parliament, and the European parliament is more of an elected consumer consultative body.

There are three problems with this structure. One is central-isation of power in the unelected bureaucracy, making it inherently vulnerable to lobbying. The second is that the European council invariably resorts to political horse-trading. The third is that the structure makes no provision for direct elections. This democratic deficit is part of the British concern.

The democratic deficit in Europe

Unease with EU remoteness can be found across Europe. Europe needs more democracy, which will give legitimacy to its legislation and curb the demands for national sovereignty. But another way to solve the democratic deficit would be to reduce the scope of the EU, which a former French president favours: the EU should get back to free trade and about ten other matters that genuinely benefit from uniform European policies. Reducing the scope of the EU would solve a perennial British complaint, that it is a super-state interfering too much in national affairs.

The democratic deficit could also be addressed, if people felt they could influence European policy. I don't remember the people being consulted about replacing single-member European parliamentary constituencies (with a typical electorate of half a million) with vast multi-member constituencies where selection is by party list and the individual's vote has little meaning. A referendum across Europe on whether to adopt direct elections to the European parliament in single-member constituencies and direct elections for commissioners would be a good start.

Leadership

The EU was designed to prevent any one state dominating, yet it is crying out for leadership. The Foundation for European Progressive Studies published a paper jointly with other European think tanks in 2013, arguing that too much was decided without political leadership or proper political debate involving the people of Europe.

Instead, European politics have been reactive, responding to events rather than shaping them. The Euro is a good example. Germany would be in a terrible state if the Euro failed, since its currency would appreciate, pricing German goods out of world markets. The International Monetary Fund, European Central Bank and European commission, now all agree that Greece needs debt relief. Germany opposes this, because as biggest creditor it would have to admit the losses.

The refugee crisis

In recent months, much has been said about how badly the EU is treating refugees from war in Syria and from insurgencies in Afghanistan, Pakistan and middle eastern and African states. This crisis is a symptom of a world with no ethics. Britain was instrumental in creating the middle eastern mess, first with the Labour government's invasion of Iraq, then with the following government's bombing of Libya and subsequently Syria. Since Britain was complicit in creating the refugee crisis, Britain should take some real responsibility for the dispossessed. Britain is abdicating its moral obligations and thereby behaving somewhat worse than the rest of the European Union.

Britain's relationship with Europe

Britain already has favourable membership terms vis-a-vis the other 27: it is not in the Euro, not in the Schengen passport-free travel area and was no longer to be bound by the concept of ever-closer union in the amended membership terms that the electorate rejected.

Britain has a representative democracy which oscillates between political extremes as different parties spend just a few years behaving like elected dictators. The rest of Europe prefers compromise and fudge. This difference is fundamental. Britain and the rest of Europe do not understand one another.

The previous government mishandled Europe. What started as "renegotiation to repatriate powers" failed at the first hurdle, since other member states would not contemplate treaty change. It then became "restricting welfare benefits" but this fell foul of the EU's anti-discrimination rules. To achieve the stated objective, denying benefits for the first four years an immigrant spends in Britain, the government would have had to refuse British citizens the same benefits for four years after reaching the age of eighteen. Policy formulation by sound bite and political opportunism hit the buffers.

Meanwhile, British civil servants have increasingly seen working in Brussels as a career dead-end, so Britain's staffing contribution to the EU bureaucracy has been dwindling. Basic mistakes about EU anti-discrimination rules resulted either from not having civil service involvement, or perhaps from not accepting advice from civil servants.

5 The state of Britain

Looked at from outside, Britain seems to be a country with a history of living an endless succession of dreams. Before 1956, Britain dreamt it was a serious power in the world; Suez put paid to that dream. Then it dreamt the pound was a world currency, while devaluation succeeded devaluation. It dreamt of perfect health care free for everyone, while rationing the NHS by queue. It dreamt of an enterprise economy yet pushed a growing debt burden on its people. Now it dreams of go-it-alone policies in a complex interconnected world. It dreams of unlimited free trade without the obligations that go with it. It dreams of improving its public services by sending key workers away. It dreams of more prosperity by disrupting one-eighth of its economy. It dreams of selling more goods than it currently can manufacture to replace the services that it sells successfully in Europe. It dreams of remaining a global capital for financial services while driving out its European financial services business. It even contemplates a complex change without breaking such a change into sensible stages.

Post-1945, Britain has slowly become a nanny state in which common sense has been replaced by elaborate rules. As shown earlier, this is a creation of the British bureaucracy, not of the EU. Leaving the EU will remove constraints on the British bureaucracy, enabling it to expand its control over citizens' lives and increase the wasteful overhead of the State.

Despite devolution, Britain has highly centralised politics. In England, the major areas of education and health are largely centralised. Centralised politics are driven by media campaigning and lobbying; the individual has little voice. Hence the disconnection between people and politics.

Politicians have always preferred the short-term fix over the long-term interests of the United Kingdom. The two-party system ensures that elected dictatorships rule for a few years, until the electorate loses faith and throws the rascals out. The result is legislation that has to be undone or amended: think identity cards for a good example. By playing to and with the media, politicians simply make bigger mistakes: Iraq is a glaring example. By allowing errors of fact to go unchallenged, politicians build the distrust that eventually is their undoing. Britain's lack of a written constitution leads to politicians endlessly fiddling with the details to gain party advantage. As examples: an unelected upper house, no devolution to England or English regions, weak local government, unequal powers between the three devolved governments.

One of the aims of this book is to redress the lack of proper information that bedevilled the EU referendum campaign. Official secrecy has to be swept away to enable politicians to be trusted by the people. Otherwise Britain will sleepwalk to the worst decline in its living standards ever as trade in goods and services suffers, employers (such as corporate Japan) depart, skilled professionals depart and public services decline. This decline will set in slowly. The time lag between the Brexit vote and the depths of recession may be five to seven years, long enough for politicians and the mass media to find some other pretext for the resulting damage.

The combination of these four factors – nanny state,

centralised politics, preference for short-term fixes over the long-term good, and complete lack of proper information – is leading to a slow build up to an existential crisis. There is a political argument that the will of the people must be respected by pursuing Brexit, in order to prevent the disconnection between the public and politicians widening. But when Britain is struggling financially, the NHS is unable to provide health care for all, and Britain's influence in the world has vanished, what will the next generation of politicians say? That it was a mess made by a previous government and nothing to do with them? The normal excuse.

Britain now needs the right solution to Brexit that preserves its trade, keeps its influence in the world and keeps the supply of professionals to support its public services. The last thing it should do is dream about future glories that may never materialise while damaging its existing European trade and integration. One-eighth of the UK economy is at stake.

Until proven otherwise by answers to the four questions posed in chapter 1, Hard Brexit appears to be a worse option than Soft Brexit. Soft Brexit, inside the EU customs union, would enable the United Kingdom to detach itself from EU institutions and the primacy of EU law apart from single market and customs union law. Therefore, Soft Brexit may be the best starting point.

Politics and the economy

Economic downturns always bring political upsets. The three-day week, which led to the fall of the Heath government, occurred in the later stages of the 1972 to 1975 recession. In downturns the old assumptions about growth, expansion and government benevolence, are discarded. Whereas a failed business threatening jobs may be bailed out in good times, in harder times the money to do so is lacking, so the business is left to fold. Unemployment rises, spending falls, and voters feel even more disillusioned.

In Britain today, the younger middle classes are burdened by debt service and repayment. Total private sector debt is at least five times GDP as a direct result of years of economic stimulus. Homes are unaffordable thanks to past policies of artificially inflating their price. The global economy is now slowing down, jobs are being lost again and the debt burden will soon matter. The past credit expansion caused economic inequality in the name of the trickle-down theory of economic growth, also known as "neo-liberalism."

Britain is no exception to the rule that political upsets are a direct result of insufficient growth or, in some cases, caused by continued economic sclerosis. Those political upsets include:

1. population displacement as a result of war, famine and disease;

2. the rise of disruptive elements on the right, such as the Tea Party and isolationists in America, UKIP in Britain, the Front Nationale in France, Golden Dawn in Greece and Jobbik in Hungary;

3. the rise of disruptive elements on the left in Greece, America and Britain;

4. the attack on immigrants, across Europe but particularly in England and Hungary.

By 2009, the British people were furious with the establishment for letting banks create dangerous products which blew up, causing the credit crunch. That fury was misplaced because banks could never have created the dangerous derivatives if government had kept the credit supply under control. What is coming, both for Britain and elsewhere, is a crisis of democracy. Another global recession, when the effects of the previous one have barely been overcome, amplified by a rush to abandon Europe that leads to a deeper downturn in Britain, will unleash a new wave of disaffection with British politicians.

Until recently, Britain has had a love affair with austerity in the belief that the books could be balanced by squeezing the poor mercilessly. Despite the warning from the referendum result, austerity by squeezing the poor may continue. The British public believe that 70% of welfare claimants are scroungers but the true figure for benefit fraud is one-hundredth of this, 0.7% – itself a good example of the lack of proper facts amplified by centralised politics allied to the media. There are two problems here. One is that almost nobody in government, the civil service, the economics profession and the national media, has any experience of abject poverty. If some of them had faced starvation and lack of opportunity, perhaps the poor would not be so mistreated now, and perhaps the poor would not be kicking back at the establishment through the ballot box. The second problem is undue official secrecy, which is why Cabinet briefing papers on Brexit must be published and the four questions set out in chapter 1 must be answered. Really open government can help get the people on side to create the national consensus the government seeks.

If we ask ourselves what Britain's place is in the world, then some uncomfortable truths appear:

1. Many in Britain believe the nation is a global giant. However, the government no longer has popular support for waging offensive military action, nor does it have the money to spend on defence. Britain does not yet have serviceable aircraft carriers and also has to hire anti-submarine patrolling aircraft from France. Does it even have the resources for basic defence of the realm?

2. Britain believes that it is an economic power, ignoring the inequalities of income and household debt on which this belief is based.

3. Britons believe that they are the fount of modern democracy, despite electing governments on a minority of votes, with scant popular support expressed through the ballot box.

The pressures caused by excessive debt are likely to mount over the next few years. Britain's elected politicians of any party will not be able to cope. Britain's public services will collapse without foreign workers, notably doctors, nurses and care workers; Britain has long failed to train enough high-quality medical professionals. It takes seven years to turn a new student into a junior doctor and another twelve to fifteen years to turn a junior doctor into a consultant. Britain will therefore need immigrant doctors for the next twenty years.

The British system of endless centralised bureaucratic agencies tripping over one another has been exposed on doctor training. In 2015, the NHS regulator for England told hospitals only to fill "essential" vacancies as most hospitals were then heading for serious financial deficits. The hospital jobs that come vacant most frequently are training placements for newly qualified doctors, since they have to serve four six-month placements before choosing whether to specialise or become General Practitioners. One-fifth of English training places were left unfilled at 1st August 2015 (one of the changeover dates) as hospitals tried to cut staffing levels. Such is the short-termism delivered by British bureaucrats, encouraged by British politicians.

Immigrant workers do bring differing training and skill levels with them. European mutual recognition directives provide for supervised periods of adjustment to handle such differences.

A spin-off from the present government's restrictions on immigration is that higher barriers are being placed on recruitment from outside the European free-movement countries. Work permits are restricted and the income level required to obtain indefinite leave to remain is being steadily increased. What will the effect be? If present visa rules for countries that are neither in the EU nor in EFTA are applied to the EU and EFTA after a Hard Brexit, then Britain will be short of workers that it desperately needs. In addition to shrinking the British economy by driving out cross-border manufacturing and services sold to the single market, Hard Brexit will shrink the British economy by adding to employment overheads and restricting recruitment.

Universities compete in a global market for the best young talent. They are concerned that they will be unable to recruit young academics and will lose pan-European funding for research. In time, this will lead to a decline in the standards achieved by British universities. But they will have a new regulator, Office for Students. Yet another "productive" overhead?

Excessive regulation always results in mediocrity. The bad may be driven out, but the good people simply go elsewhere. Britain needs to end its cult of uniformity and the mediocrity that follows from it. The one shining exception, Britain's Olympic success, happened because UK Sport was ruthless about merit.

The disconnection between citizens and the political elite

One of the themes that came through time and time again from people interviewed or participating in EU referendum panel discussions was that they blamed immigrants for NHS queues. But those queues are the result of austerity, not of immigration, perhaps aided by Britain's addiction to centralised finance with resources allocated by arbitrary funding formulae. And free movement only relates to nationals of the 27 other EU member states plus the four EFTA countries; European immigration is not total immigration.

If the less well-off are to be persuaded to put Britain first, they need a stake in Britain. They were stamped on by the previous government's austerity policies, which hurt the poor far more than those comfortably off. Instead of pursuing corporation tax cuts, the Chancellor should cancel the bedroom tax, ease the requirements for fitness for work assessments, and ease the cuts imposed through the back door of universal benefit. Then people may feel less inclined to give the government a kicking. The poor have borne an unfair share of austerity. Britain needs less dividing lines and more cooperation.

Parts of England need to change their attitude to Scotland, Northern Ireland, Gibraltar and expatriates, recognising that their views may be different but do matter. Who spoke for Northern Ireland, Gibraltar and expatriates in the EU referendum campaign? The previous prime minister did have a plan to draw media attention to Gibraltar but his intended visit was cancelled following the murder of Jo Cox MP.

The British political system is built upon divisions between parties and opposition from the other side, thereby entrenching divisions. The differences between parties are a century out of date. A start could be made when rebuilding both Lords and Commons by adopting circular chambers, instead of perpetuating opposing benches. Their inhabitants need to stop arguing like kids and get together to fix Britain.

The world economy is struggling, thanks to the debt burden created by politicians over the past seventy-odd years. A nation can only prosper if its skill level is high and it competes vigorously for business. Citizens barely understand how their bread is earned. Skill levels are low, thanks to educational neglect of non-academic teenagers.

Britain's poverty problem is as much poverty of education in a challenging world as lack of job opportunities. What has Britain done? Sacrificed further education and public libraries to austerity. Corporation tax cuts are no solution to lack of skills.

Lack of skills and a home-grown nanny state with top-heavy bureaucracy are Britain's own problems to solve; they are not caused by the EU. Lack of knowledge of what the EU does for Britons follows from lack of education.

Britain is in its current predicament because some claims made in the referendum campaign have proved difficult to verify. Now the official line is that 23rd June 2016 was a once-in-a-generation referendum. Politicians are scared of deep-ening the lack of trust that citizens have in them and have achieved a sullen acquiescence from the 48%, the biggest single group when taking account of the divisions between the different groups of leavers. Britain is now in a twilight state where the economic damage is inevitable but not yet happening and therefore not showing in statistics. Unemployment is always a lagging indicator of the state of the economy, and job losses will start on a serious scale following an announcement of Hard Brexit. Triggering Article 50 without stating what the government intends to achieve will be worse because it will maximise business uncertainty.

Referendums in Britain

The conduct of referendums needs to change. What happened prior to 23rd June 2016 was a national disgrace.

The EU referendum was largely conducted by media posturing over too long a time period. In any future referendum, complete information must be provided, together with impartial analysis, direct to each voter, not through filters and amplifiers chosen by the media. Providing facts requires a balanced review process, beyond the capabilities of campaigning politicians.

The UK Statistics Authority twice protested about the statement that £350 million a week would be saved by leaving the EU. Vote Leave ignored them and carried on repeating the error. Much of the press ignored the evidence and carried on quoting it, instead of burying it. TV and radio allowed the story to be repeated.

Where were the Electoral Commission in all this? They counted the pennies after they had been spent, to ensure that spending limits were not breached. Spending limits are irrelevant if you can get free airtime in "discussions" and thereby broadcast insufficiently researched opinions. Politicians excluded media coverage and truth in politics from the Electoral Commission's remit. Shame on them.

If Britain is ever to get out of the habit of digging holes for itself then falling into them, it will need an electoral process, including referendums, that values truth, facts and objective analysis above spin, lies and failure to do homework. The one abiding message from both Brexit and Iraq is that politicians rarely do their homework. Their love of campaigning takes precedence. They are still campaigning, trying to sell the public a dream that has no grounding in fact. Britain has already lost credibility and influence in the world thanks to Iraq. Both major parties have now been complicit in damaging Britain.

Here are some new ideas about how to conduct British referendums:

1. Vote Leave objected to the government sending out a pro-EU leaflet. However, what was needed and nobody

provided was a careful analysis of what leaving the EU would mean: what would be the effect on trade, what else would change, what would the options be? The Leave campaign did not even say what options they proposed. Remain were too occupied with political campaigning to provide enough facts to the electorate about European trade and cooperation. An electorate lacking facts cannot be expected to make a complex judgement.

2. While the government's proposed abolition of the 15-year expatriate voting restriction is welcome, the many British citizens who have never lived in the UK should be allowed to vote. Here's an idea: in UK-wide elections and referendums, combine expatriates with Gibraltar to make an electoral group of those resident outside the British Isles. This would be a counterweight to England, which currently dominates UK elections. How about creating expatriate constituencies managed centrally instead of every local council having to keep track of voters all over the world? British citizens could then stand on a platform of representing expatriate interests, bringing their broader view to the legislative process.

3. There needs to be a majority of the nations as well as a simple majority of the votes for a referendum to pass. Given the potential break-up of the United Kingdom and dishonourable treatment of Gibraltar/expatriates, it should be easy to devise a second threshold of a majority of the five groups, i.e. the four nations plus expatriates and Gibraltarians. Therefore a referendum would only be valid if at least three out of the five groups, England, Scotland,

Wales, Northern Ireland and citizens living outside the British Isles, had a majority. Absent the dual majority of votes and nations/groups, the existing position would continue unchanged.

4. 16 and 17 year-olds should be allowed to vote. If they were able to express an opinion on independence in the 2014 Scottish referendum, why could they not vote in the EU referendum? Such referendums are about the future of the young, not the prejudices of their elders.

5. In this day and age, sending voting forms around the world by post is Victorian. One lady in Australia was reported as receiving her referendum papers on the morning of 23rd June. The papers included instructions to make sure they were returned to her council offices in the UK by 10 pm on 23rd June. The government is very keen for you to do everything by Internet to save it money, except for expatriate voting rights which are stymied.

Britain's future

Britain cannot afford to throw its existing EU trade, sales of services and cross-border manufacturing, together accounting for one-eighth of its economy, on the scrap heap. Nor can it afford to split the nations further, either by neglecting Scotland, Northern Ireland, Gibraltar and expatriates, or by adopting a Hard Brexit solution that only a minority desire.

For the UK to have a prosperous future outside the EU, it should stay in the single market with or without the EU customs union. The referendum result could also be honoured by a closer

Association agreement, but this would either need extensive diplomacy before the formal exit negotiations can start, or an interim stage in the single market and customs union.

A national consensus requires more than talking to large businesses, local councils, devolved governments and industry lobbying groups. It requires all citizens to be involved in understanding the issues, no matter what view they took on 23rd June 2016. A rushed consultation through trade bodies is woefully inadequate: it does not ask the **population** what they want.

Brexit is being promoted by political salespeople as a national opportunity to embrace the world beyond Europe. Even contemplating taking Britain out of the single market is an act of economic vandalism that will return to haunt a future government. Rational decisions need to replace mass emotions. A national consensus requires truly open, honest government and wide understanding of relevant facts.

6 What now?

This book has produced evidence that Hard Brexit will not be advantageous to the United Kingdom. The only solution that avoids immediate economic damage commencing soon after Article 50 is invoked, and has a realistic chance of being implemented in two years, will be Soft Brexit inside the customs union.

It is possible to reach this conclusion by a simple hierarchy of decisions:

1. Do the answers to the four questions posed in chapter 1 show that it is beneficial to give up European free trade amounting to 12.9% of the British economy?

If this proposition can be demonstrated to be true, contrary to all the evidence in this book, then Britain can abandon the single market and lose a major part of one-eighth of the economy.

If the answer is "Yes" your choice is: **Hard Brexit.**

If the answer is "No", go on to question 2.

2. Is it more important to control European immigration, which currently amounts to only 5% of the population in Britain, rather than maintain European trade amounting to 12.9% of the economy?

If the answer is "Yes" your choice is: **Hard Brexit.**

If the answer is "No", go on to question 3.

3. Should Britain abandon cross-border manufacturing and hurt its agricultural exports, for somewhat lesser economic damage? There will still be interim losses before new trade agreements can take effect.

If the answer is "Yes" your choice is: **Soft Brexit outside the customs union.**

If the answer is "No", go on to question 4.

4. If questions 1, 2 and 3 all produced "No" as an answer:

Your choice is: **Soft Brexit inside the customs union.**

5. However, if the UK wants a closer relationship with the EU:

Your choice is: **a Close Association agreement** *(but be prepared for* **Soft Brexit inside the customs union** *as an interim solution while negotiations continue).*

Whether the government chooses to make its own decision, conduct a national consultation, hold a further referendum, or call a general election, these are the decisions that need to be taken in order to choose which form of Brexit to adopt. The priority is to secure what Britain's future relationship with the

EU should be and to unify the majority of British citizens around that chosen relationship. The one conclusion that is unavoidable from the analysis in this book is: no Hard Brexit without a ratified trade agreement and the informed consent of the British people first.

Because the trade figures have been misunderstood, politicians believe their own lie: that Britain will get a good deal because they think the EU needs Britain more than Britain needs the EU. The phrase "post-truth politics" says it all. The trade to GDP ratios tell a different story. Britain is dependent on the single market for one-eighth of its economy, or more, whereas the average dependence of all the remaining 27 member states on their exports to the UK is 3.1% of their individual economies.

Britain does not recognise how weak its negotiating position is. A serious error. British politicians misread the trade balance because they do not understand the Rotterdam effect and the "all or nothing" nature of passported services. Another serious error. Apart from not understanding the data, it seems that governing politicians are making the mistake of treating the other 27 member states as if they were one single country simply because they negotiate as one. Wrong, wrong and wrong again.

British politicians are now in a trap of their own devising. The twenty-seven remaining member states in the EU feel let down by Britain and will no longer behave as colleagues or allies. Start negotiations believing that Britain has a strong hand, then Britain will be the loser. Single-market access will then be exactly as it is for over 100 countries that are neither in the EEA nor have trade agreements with the EU: tariffs, quotas and customs checks for manufactured goods, with Britain's European service businesses largely shut down. Forget all the arguments about the Euro, about the super-state, about the primacy of EU law. **The one jewel in the crown that Britain so far has exploited to its benefit has been the single market.**

Election timetables, whether in Europe or the United Kingdom, should not be allowed to dictate events. British politicians must put the British national interest ahead of the electoral cycles. Obviously, any solution must provide for maintaining or increasing employment, not destroying it. This requires standing firm both against demands from the EU to get on with giving notice and also demands from some elements in Britain that they alone possess the "right" solution and electoral mandate that must be implemented immediately.

The poisonous politics of immigration have been allowed too much influence. Applying logic to the referendum result, the majority would support staying in the single market with only a minority desiring Hard Brexit. Therefore the nation can be united by staying in the single market, or divided by Hard Brexit.

Some voters blamed immigrants for the damage done by austerity. Given all the populism, it should be clear that a proportion of those voters were wrongly informed. An honest admission that austerity caned the poor, to the benefit of the well-off, would put an end to this misunderstanding.

Putting immigration control first may yet be the worst mistake made by a post-1945 British government. Given the disarray in the Labour party, there is a temptation to call an early general election. Using an increased majority to force Hard Brexit would ensure that chickens will come home to roost when the damage materialises in the next and next-but-one parliaments. Such wilful destruction of the British economy and possibly of the United Kingdom would finish the Conservative party. Why? Because shutting down passported financial services in Britain will hit the middle classes hardest. Like the rebellion from the North caused by austerity, a middle-class rebellion concentrated in cities and university towns will have electoral consequences. Affected businesses will stop providing political support through donations. Irrespective of the national polls, marginal constituencies, with a high proportion of Remain voters, will not vote for a party choosing Hard Brexit.

Let's recap on the immigration issues, which have appeared throughout this book. Remember that the EU makes the rules but they apply throughout the EEA and, in the case of free movement, the rules apply to all four EFTA countries. Treating the referendum result as an instruction from the people to control European immigration at the expense of jobs is wrong because:

1. The referendum question only asked if voters wished to leave the EU. Immigration was not part of the question. Some of the 52% voting leave only wanted to end the supremacy of EU law, and some wanted to stay in the single market.

2. The wealth creators will be driven out, and elderly expatriates needing support will return to Britain.

3. Immigrants from Europe are mainly younger workers paying taxes, bringing skills that Britain lacks and enabling

Britain to support its post-1945 baby boomers who are now retiring.

4. Politicians should not allow immigration to take the blame for the damage done to the poor by austerity, nor should they put sectional party needs for votes ahead of the national interest.

5. The official immigration and EU population statistics are inconsistent. It is possible that EU immigration is being overstated.

6. Since the EU is not going to compromise over the fundamental principle of free movement, Britain faces a stark choice between allowing free movement and destroying jobs. Britain needs the single market four times as much as the average EU member state needs Britain.

It is *possible* but unlikely that some sort of token compromise over free movement might emerge. However, Switzerland is not a role model. Britain is in a completely different situation from Switzerland, a country that is neither in the EU nor the EEA. One quarter of the population of Switzerland is not Swiss; Britain is objecting to just 5% of its population being EU nationals. The proposed "Swiss compromise" gives EU/EEA residents in Switzerland equal rights with Swiss nationals and does not impose any quotas or limits on free movement. There is no solution here.

Opinion polls already show that a majority of the public want to stay in the single market. If the government of the United

Kingdom continues to insist on Hard Brexit then the people will need to speak again. There are only three way to do this: a parliamentary vote, a general election or another referendum. In a general election, parties must state whether they will keep Britain in the single market or go for Hard Brexit. In a referendum, the question must be unambiguous and worded so that few politicians will dare to tell lies. A suitable question could be:

In order to implement the decision to leave the EU, Britain has to choose between staying in the single market on the same terms as 30 other countries or damaging one-eighth of the economy with little prospect of replacement jobs for at least ten years. Do you want to:

Put people out of work? ☐

Stay in the single market on the same terms as 30 other countries? ☐

The two biggest problems in Europe are lack of leadership and the democratic deficit. Britain could have led a reform campaign; sadly, it has chosen to take to the sidelines. Like it or not, the EU has been a force for economic prosperity and peaceful co-operation across Europe.

Appendix: Examples of political misconceptions

Table 7 lists those political mistakes and misconceptions used in Britain's EU referendum campaign, that are discussed in this book. It is essential to read the detailed text in order to understand the extent to which they are mistakes, misconceptions or simply unknowns. The list is not exhaustive.

Claim, innuendo or implication
Agreements such as between the EU and Canada are for free trade
Britain can have free trade with the EU and control immigration
Britain can stop sending £350m a week to the EU
Britain can regain its sovereignty
Britain will get a better trade deal with the EU than it has now
Britain will do better on its own
Our trade is held back by the EU
The EU needs Britain
Britain does not need the EU
Britons living in the EU/EFTA will have the right to remain and EU/EFTA nationals working in the UK can continue to do so, under the Vienna convention
There will be less regulation outside the EU
We will negotiate favourable exit terms

Table 7: Mistakes in the referendum campaign

Table 8 gives a small number of examples of continuing mistakes that are discussed in the text. There will be others. These examples show that the inability of campaigning politicians to do their homework may now be affecting government:

Claim	Reality
Equivalence rules will enable Britain to continue to trade freely with the EEA, with full single-market access	The EU will not allow equivalence for more than a few business sectors, as this would enable the UK to avoid budget contributions and free-movement obligations.
We will get a good trade deal because Germany sells more cars in Britain than elsewhere.	High earning jobs will move to other countries, so German cars will be sold in those countries instead of in Britain.
The common travel area with the Irish Republic existed before 1973 and will continue.	The Irish Republic joined the EU with Britain but is not leaving with Britain. Britain will itself terminate the common travel area if it leaves the customs union.
Britain can copy the proposed Swiss solution to free movement and immigration control.	The Swiss solution does not restrict inward migration and grants equal rights to EEA citizens resident in Switzerland.

Table 8: Examples of continuing mistakes

Sparkling Books

We publish:

Crime, mystery, thriller, suspense, horror and romance

YA fiction

Non-fiction

All titles are also available as e-books from your e-book retailer.

For current list of titles visit:

www.sparklingbooks.com

@SparklingBooks